Fellini's Casanova

SCRIPT AND DIRECTOR
Series Editor Inga Karetnikova

Fellini's Casanova

by Federico Fellini
(in collaboration with Bernardino Zapponi)

Translated from the Italian by Claudia Cremasco
(with special thanks to Oren Mc Cleary)

HEINEMANN
Portsmouth, NH

Heinemann
A division of Reed Elsevier Inc.
361 Hanover Street
Portsmouth, NH 03801-3912
Offices and agents throughout the world

The author and publisher are grateful for permission to reprint previously published material: Excerpt from *Orlando Furioso, Part 1* by Ludovico Ariosto, translated by Barbara Reynolds. Copyright © 1975 by Barbara Reynolds. Published by Penguin Books Ltd. Reprinted by permission of David Higham Associates, London.

Library of Congress Cataloging-in-Publication Data

Fellini, Federico.
    [Casanova. English]
    Fellini's Casanova / by Federico Fellini (in collaboration with Bernardino Zapponi) : translated from the Italian by Claudia Cremasco.
    p.   cm. -- (Script and director)
    Translated from Italian.
    ISBN 0-435-07020-7
    I. Zapponi, Bernardino.   II. Casanova (Motion picture)
III. Title.   IV. Series.
PN1997.C3524   1997
791.43′72--dc21
                                    97-5393
                                        CIP

Printed in the United States of America on acid-free paper
01 00 99 98 97   DA   1 2 3 4 5 6

Contents

Foreword

Fellini's Casanova is the most personal of the director's films. Granted, all Fellini's films are personal. Still, *Fellini's Casanova* is a special case. This becomes even more intriguing if we remember that Fellini, while making the film, used every opportunity to condemn Giacomo Casanova. He called him "a dull writer, a troublemaker, a braggart, an arsehole, a megalomaniac, a fascist, a lover with ice-cold sperm, a human piston, a jumping jack, a provincial playboy, and a blockhead." In fact, he verbally abused Casanova so much that it prompted Gore Vidal (who at one point was asked to revise the script) to remind Fellini of the old artistic axiom that one cannot create a genuine work of art about a character one despises. Fellini ignored the reminder and continued his verbal attacks, only to call the film, when it was finished, his "most complete, expressive and courageous" work.

But is it important that Fellini despised Giacomo Casanova? The question is relevant because what he *said* about Casanova and what we *see* on the screen are actually two different things. In fact, we can even say that *Fellini's Casanova* has little to do with the real-life Casanova — an eighteenth-century Venetian rake who breathed, bragged, swindled, fornicated, filled four thousand pages with his memoirs, and then died, dissolute and pathetic, in (a Venetian's nightmare) some snow-covered, little, provincial place.

There is an opinion that Fellini made *Fellini's Casanova* almost accidentally. One prominent critic even suggested that the film "was born from a signature placed without caution on a contract proposed without caution." Actually, Fellini never made a film he didn't want to make, and no amount of begging or bribery on the part of a producer could convince him to change his mind. As Bernardino Zapponi, Fellini's collaborator on the film's script, put it: "Fellini won't accept a compromise. Even if he starved, he would continue on his own way."

The production of *Fellini's Cassanova* was plagued with problems right from the start: two producers, De Laurentiis and Rizzoli, abandoned the project one after the other; and the third, Grimaldi, had a hugely publicized falling-out with Fellini, which had to be resolved in court. In short, Fellini had plenty of chances to "jump ship." But no, he tenaciously clung to it. Besides, he started working on *Fellini's Casanova* in 1974, immediately after having finished *Amarcord*, which was such an instant critical and commercial success that Fellini could, at that time, make almost any film he wished. He was fifty-four years old. And he wished to make his Casanova.

One thing must be clarified. Despite constant tabloid "revelations," Fellini, in his own personal life, was *not* a Casanova. True, he was curious about women, genuinely loved and admired them, and had a lot of women friends. He was very affectionate, but, according to Zapponi, if a relationship threatened to go too far, he would terminate it. "I would think he would say, 'How can I leave Giulietta?' [Giulietta Masina, to whom Fellini was married for 50 years.]"

The film's production scope was enormous, even by Fellini's standards. It called for seventy-two sets (later cut to fifty-four), which included palaces and canals of eighteenth-century Venice, an island in the Venetian lagoon, apartments of Parisian aristocrats, the Royal Theater in Dresden, a harem in Constantinople, streets in Amsterdam, the river Thames and a fantastic circus in London, Voltaire's Villa in Geneva, a castle in Bohemia, and so on. Fellini built all of these in the indoor studio (the famous Cinecittá in Rome), in order, as he said, to have *absolute control* over every aspect of the visual image. In addition, he insisted that only authentic fabrics be used for more than three thousand costumes for his extras, and that all these fabrics be dyed with the same organic dyes as those used in the eighteenth-century.

Fellini didn't want fakes. He was recreating reality—albeit, the reality of his imagination.

And precisely for that reason, he chose a tall, lanky Canadian, Donald Sutherland, for the lead role. "He has an ideal face for the part," Fellini explained, "absent features, a hazy, watery look with something shapeless about it . . . . That 'moonface' of his is completely alien to the image people have of Casanova: the dark-eyed, magnetic Italian with raven locks and dark skin. And since I want to turn the traditional model upside down, a face like that is exactly what I need."

So, what *is* the traditional model? Who was the *real* Giacomo Casanova?

He was born in Venice in 1725, the son of actors (an occupation that was as much admired by the eighteenth-century public while *inside* the theater as it was despised while *outside* of it), but he claimed that his father had actually descended from the Spanish nobility, with one ancestor having been the private secretary to the king. In case this claim wouldn't fly, he hinted that his mother, a cobbler's daughter, had had an affair with a Venetian patrician, and that he, Giacomo, was the result. Later in life, he even adopted a phony title—Chevalier de Seingalt.

Giacomo was a quick study, and by the age of twenty-four he had been a preacher, a lawyer, a mercenary officer, a quack physician, a fiddler, a publisher, and an accomplished cardsharp. He was slim, athletic, swarthy and hawklike. "He would have been very handsome had he not been ugly," wrote his friend, Prince de Ligne. He was a good shot, a witty storyteller, and an even better listener—a quality rather useful in establishing friendships.

He had a smattering of metaphysics and mathematics, could recite Ariosto and quote Cicero, and felt equally at ease in ducal palaces and in gambling dens. For more than forty years he moved constantly from country to country—Paris, Madrid, Vienna, London, Zurich, Munich, Amsterdam, Warsaw, St. Petersburg, Nice, Parma, Constantinople, Paris again—never staying in one place for more than a few months. He would undertake anything. To the King of France, he proposed to organize a state lottery to improve France's finances; and to the Duke of Wiirttemberg he proposed to fortify the duke's capital. He conversed on economy with Catherine the Great and on philosophy with Voltaire.

He wrote a play, an opus on Homer, and a treatise on geometry. He was an opera impresario, and a journalist, and at one point he ruined himself financially by self-publishing his excruciatingly long futuristic novel. But he knew how to reimburse himself by making murky "cabalistic" pronouncements (he dabbled in necromancy and black magic as well) before some titled fools, or, aided by his nimble fingers and long, lace-trimmed sleeves, by successfully playing faro—his favorite game. Then again, he squandered money as easily as he swindled it.

He was a connoisseur of many arts, *including* the art of seduction. He liked all women—maids, duchesses, nuns, courtesans, peasants, underaged girls, aging matrons—and he didn't mind incest.

Toward the end of his life, the impoverished librarian to a provincial Bohemian nobleman, Casanova set out to write his memoirs. When he died in 1798 at the age of seventy-three, he left thousands of sheets filled on both sides with his large, clear handwriting, recounting his life in minute detail (he had a remarkable memory), the folio sheets bursting with hundreds of episodes and picaresque characters.

In his memoirs, Casanova is a scholar, a philosopher, a scientist, a poet, a skillful gambler, an impresario, a publisher, an interlocutor with kings and wits, a financier, and an expert on cabala. In his film, Fellini completely ignores all these activities, focusing exclusively on Casanova's relations with women. And then, whether the real Casanova was a brilliant man, as he had claimed himself to be, or, essentially, a scoundrel, as Fellini repeatedly asserted, becomes totally irrelevant, because Fellini's Casanova is an *invention,* and *not* Giacomo Casanova.

Fellini, almost literally, molded Sutherland into the image he envisioned. In the makeup room, the actor's hairline was shaved several inches up along his scalp, to greatly enlarge his forehead; his nose and chin were rebuilt; his eyes, eyebrows, and mouth were reshaped. And Fellini, standing in the darkness behind the camera, with Sutherland under the floodlights, directed the actor's every movement, step, gesture, and glance. He would mime a fleeting smile, a shade of a melancholy expression, or slightly flip his hand, and the actor, almost without looking, would instantly mirror it. Sutherland, known as independent and opinionated, submitted totally to Fellini. When asked about this, he replied, "Why resist? The man's a genius." Then he added, "It is as if he paints an extraordinary flower and then says [to me] crawl into it and make the petals move."

Only once while making the film did Fellini make an attempt to approach the real Casanova, though he did it in a peculiar way. He went to see Gustavo Rol, a well-known medium and psychic living in Turin, and asked Rol to contact Casanova's ghost for him. Rol, a harsh old man of Scandinavian extraction, obliged, held a séance and, according to Fellini, was able to summon the ghost. Casanova was rather unfriendly, and he addressed Fellini as Signor Goldoni, a Venetian dramatist of his time. Rol then produced several sheets of unintelligible scribbling—Casanova's supposed ideas for Fellini's film. Upon leaving, Fellini found in his pocket Casanova's calling card, with one laconic sentence of apparently sexual advice scrawled on it: "Never on your feet; never after eating." The encounter was clearly unsatisfactory.

In the film, Casanova is constantly on the move; his perpetual goal is to seduce yet another woman. His success is almost inevitable. As a good-luck charm, he always carries with him a small wooden box that contains a wind-up toy—an erect gilded bird. And every time the consummation begins, the bird flutters; flaps its wings; and, accompanied by high-pitched, hypnotic music, starts pumping up and down in its pediment, mimicking Casanova's pumping in bed. Casanova works hard: his body tense, his forehead sweaty, his eyes glossy; convulsing, he reaches a climax. The bird stops momentarily, then flutters its wings, and begins again its rhythmic movements. Casanova resumes his strenuous cold gymnastics.

Only twice in his travels does he fall in love, both times unhappily. First, with a cello player named Henriette, a mysterious French girl, who abandons him, leaving him devastated. The second time, with Isabella, the ravishing daughter of a Genevan scientist, who nurses him out of a grave illness, but declines kindly his passionate declaration of love.

Then, at the Court of Württemberg, he encounters Rosalba, the woman of his dreams—calm and breathtakingly beautiful. Alas, she is not real. She is a life-sized mechanical doll; a wonder of the world, made by a genius master.

Smitten, Casanova carries her into his bedroom, and there, tenderly, he makes love to her. "I love you, I love you," he mutters, tears running down his cheeks. The sinister gilded bird, his pumping alter ego, is not with him now.

At the end of the film, the old Casanova has a dream: he is back in his beloved Venice; he is young again, dancing slowly with Rosalba over the frozen Grand Canal. She is the only one who understands him. The other women of his life, in their silk gowns, like birds of Paradise, appear for a moment, and then glide away over the ice, while he keeps dancing with Rosalba, until both of them fade into the void.

Disregarding what Fellini said about the real Casanova, *his* Casanova is *not* a scoundrel. He might be foolish or naughty, but he is also generous, melancholy, sensitive. Yes, he is sometimes manipulative—he uses women, but they use him too—and with all the women in the world available to him, he is deeply, heart-wrenchingly unhappy. It is as if the women he beds are too "corporeal" for him and he is forever searching for *the* woman—the ideal creation that does not exist. Rosalba, the enchanting mechanical doll, comes closest to it.

And so, *who* is this fascinating apparition—Fellini's Casanova? An incurable idealist, longing for the unattainable? Then why, as Fellini's assistant recalled, did the director mutter while shooting the film, "I should never have made this film. I should have let it go"? Could it be that Fellini made the film at a time when he was going through the stage in his life akin to what Tolstoy went through when he was writing his "Kreutzer Sonata"? Fellini almost said that: "For me the film meant crossing the line, gliding into the last part of my life . . . . Perhaps, subconsciously I placed all my fears, the anxiety I can't face in this film." The anxiety of the artist who is always expected to perform; a "vanity of vanities!" anxiety; the anxiety of ultimate loneliness; the anxiety of the void—encroaching and inescapable. "*Casanova* is a pretext for a conversation with a spectator, as are many other films of mine, in this case even more so," Fellini said. Now it is up to the spectators to discern in *Fellini's Casanova* what each is ready for—which, in essence, is the case with every great work of art.

Leon Steinmetz

Preface

When Fellini was pursuing Marcello Mastroianni to play the protagonist of his *La Dolce Vita*, he was perpetually thwarted in his production planning because Marcello, unreasonably, wanted to read a script before he would commit to the project. A script was promised him each tomorrow until Marcello Mastroianni finally told Federico Fellini that the tomorrow had all gone by and that if the script wasn't there by the end of the afternoon, he, Marcello, would take another project. That afternoon, two Roman swarthies pushed a huge, eight-by-ten-foot parcel through his apartment door. Under the hemp ties and brown paper was a perfect, pastel cartoon revealing a naked Marcello in a black fedora sitting in a lotus position on a Magritte surface of endless water, his sexual organ dangling a good seven feet into the depths where, swimming in circles all around the tip, were three beautiful, Botticelliesque mermaids . . . Marcello signed.

That was Federico's script. He didn't want anything more concretely anchored in the imaginations of others than something as ephemeral as that: the truth, but not the fact. He didn't look at dailies, at rushes, while we were shooting *Casanova*. He didn't want his ever-fluid, three-dimensional fantasy stilled by its two-dimensional representation.

He felt much the same about the written word. It was there to be changed; at once a conceit and a deceit, an indication for set designers, the costumiers, and the financiers. The written word was for him a participating piece in his game of avoiding the decisive artistic reality until finally the reality crushed relentlessly its birthright upon him.

The battle liberated him.

With us, the liberation came with the mechanical doll.

The heart of the film revealed itself to him there, by the fireplace, while she and I danced in front of him. Frantically, he scribbled down notes for the just-then-thought-of-moment with her on the ice of eternity—the end of the picture.

Fellini floated through those scenes enchanted with his perfection, transported by the bliss of its beauty. So satisfied was he that paranoia and mischief drained away from him. Purity of vision sat as solid as mercury in his soul. Peace and tranquillity reigned.

It was a very, very beautiful time.

Sweet music drummed from his fingers.

He sat on my knee and smiled all the time.

The script that had often been *uno duo tre quattro cinque* now lounged in constant conversation with him.

It danced with the mechanical girl.

The words were picked like grapes and burst into the mouths of words said earlier.

The script was overlaid, scattered over the film like strewn flowers.

A creation whose words erupted after nine months of patient shooting.

It felt like a miracle, an epiphany.

When he had cut it all together and we quietly walked arm in arm in Fregene, he confided to me in the evening shadows that it seemed to him that this was his best, his most satisfying work.

He was thrilling, quite literally, breathtaking, to be with.

Donald Sutherland

FELLINI'S CASANOVA

In the darkness of the screen a voice is heard:

CASANOVA (*V. O.*): I am Giacomo Casanova, knight of Seingalt. From Venice. I was born in Venice in 1725. My mother was the famous actress Zanetta. I am descended from a very ancient family. I've never had any bearing. I let myself go where the wind drove me. Remembering the pleasures I've had I can feel them yet again, and I laugh at the sorrows I once bore since I suffer them no longer . . . I have had all four temperaments: the phlegmatic, the sanguine, the choleric, and the melancholy. By adapting my diet to my constitution I have always enjoyed good health. Feeling that I was born for those of the other sex, I've always loved women and made them love me as much as possible . . . Above all I loved my city, ancient and bright, cruel and tender, yielding . . .

EXT. STREET AND SQUARES OF THE 18th CENTURY VENICE DURING THE CARNIVAL. NIGHT.

The big square, the streets all around seem to be deserted. Yet there is an atmosphere of waiting and suspense.

From the distance we hear drums, and other instruments with dissonant and odd sounds. They get closer. Here and there the first queer MASKED FIGURES appear, popping out from the streets and the canals or coming up from the gondolas. There are maskers of every kind: HARLEQUINS,

PUNCHES, HORSES HEADS, DEVILS, DRAGONS . . . Little by little a big crowd gathers. They dance, jumping to a certain rhythm, all together, and start to move toward the Grand Canal. Many ropes converge on the middle of the Canal, forming a tangle that looks like a sail boat, or a net. At a signal the ropes are pulled all at once, and the wooden head of a colossal woman, the symbol of Venice, appears. It emerges gradually. It seems that her eyes stare out in bewilderment.

A PIERROT in white clothes and with white heavily powdered face watches the crowd with lively interest. This is Casanova. A WOMAN approaches him—we don't see her face—and hands him a note.

The gigantic head is not yet completely out of the water, when some ropes break and the head sinks into the Canal amid the crowd's laughter and screams.

INT. CONVENT. PARLOR. NIGHT.

The room is spacious. The NUNS are preparing it for a feast which is about to begin. They move long benches against the wall, set a long table for the refreshments: desserts and cakes which are very elaborate, tortuous, baroque. Up in a gallery, behind a large grating, are seated the NUNS who will play to accompany the dances; one is at the harp, another at the organ, one has a cello, the last, a violin. A NUN who has been on lookout screams, excited and scared at the same time:

NUN: Here they are!

The NUNS all together, like a flock of swallows, run away. They scatter, running to hide. From behind the gratings, they peep out in a throbbing movement of veils. A crowd of MASKERS enters in the parlor, laughing, singing, turning somersaults. There is a BRIGHELLA, who has a huge rubber syringe, with which he's poking a Harlequin's bottom; a PUNCH eating pasta from a chamber pot with his hands; a boasting CAPTAIN MATAMAROS with a big sword. One HARLEQUIN, for a joke, touches the Captain's genitals with a show of admiration.

The NUNS behind the gratings look down at them laughing.

CASANOVA-PIERROT enters. His large cap and the white hat band cover half of his face. He is skipping, staggering, with a foolish gait.

The other MASKERS make room for him, applauding.

VOICES: A Pierrot! ... It's very rare to see one in Venice ...

The musician NUNS, up behind the gratings, strike up a minuet that has the sad grace of church music. Couples throw themselves into the dance. CASANOVA-PIERROT grabs by her waist a woman dressed as a Harlequin and starts dancing with this HARLEQUINESS.

The MASKERS move faster and faster, turning somersaults and pirouettes. The musician NUNS speed up the tempo. They too are seized by a sort of sensual exaltation.

CASANOVA-PIERROT, all sweaty—his white costume is in fact covered with stains—is dancing with HARLEQUINESS without resting. A jealous HARLEQUIN, laughing, hits Casanova's head with his stick. CASANOVA-PIERROT turns, grabs him by his waist, lifts him up and hurls him to the ground. The MASKERS stop dancing, looking around now at the scene, laughing. They throw themselves into the fray. Although it is just a game, there's something fierce and violent about it.

The NUNS behind the gratings, laugh gleefully. Suddenly an ABBOT enters. He claps his hands to calm them down, as if he were a schoolmaster.

ABBOT: Ladies, gentlemen, friends ... Let's not forget to give to God what belongs to God. After pleasure, some atonement. Come everyone, follow me to the chapel ...

The ABBOT sets out, and all the MASKERS, now calm and contrite, follow him.

EXT. SHORE OF THE SMALL ISLAND SAN BARTOLO. NIGHT.

CASANOVA, in his Pierrot costume, is on the shore. He holds a candle, and by the candlelight, is reading aloud a note:

CASANOVA: "A nun who has been watching you every Sunday for two months at the convent church would like to meet you. She will wait for you on San Bartolo's shore. Come by yourself, without a servant, and hold a candle in your hand . . ."

CASANOVA looks around anxiously. Suddenly, in the flickering candle light, he catches the sight of a gondola which is approaching. Inside there's someone, standing still. It seems to be a man. CASANOVA frowns. He suspects it may be a trap. But as the gondola comes closer, it's clear the person aboard is a woman wearing male clothes; it is the nun, MADDALENA. She's smiling in a radiant, enigmatic way.

INT. DE BERNIS'S VILLA. NIGHT.

In rapid succession flash by entrance, hall, long elegant corridor. MADDALENA, very young and beautiful, gently holding CASANOVA's hand, shows him the way. They enter the lodge. It is an octagonal room completely covered with mirrors on walls and ceiling. Everything is reflected there—it looks like a kaleidoscope. The room's white marble fireplace is encrusted with Chinese porcelain tiles with graphic erotic scenes on them. CASANOVA, fascinated, is observing everything. He turns to MADDALENA.

CASANOVA: My love, let me slip these clothes off you; they are too severe for our merry encounter!
MADDALENA: Just a moment; we ought to wait. My friend hasn't arrived yet.

CASANOVA takes a step back in astonishment.

CASANOVA: Your friend?
MADDALENA: Mr. De Bernis, my lover. He's lent us this lodge, but in return he wants to be present, without being seen.

CASANOVA bursts out laughing.

CASANOVA: Ah, that's rich! Well, this will add a different flavor. But where will this eccentric man find room?

MADDALENA shows him a small door with a hole in it. She opens the door into a changing room with a small elegant bed, an armchair, a small table and chair, and everything else one might need: a lighted lamp, some bottles of spirits, glasses, water, a snuff box.

MADDALENA: He will sit here. If your performance is good, he won't be bored!

CASANOVA: It will be. Moreover, I'll be very polite.

MADDALENA: Why, no! Whenever did passionate lovers mind manners?

CASANOVA: Well then, I'll only be delicate.

MADDALENA: Lovely.

She stops, pricks up her ears, then winks to signal that her friend has arrived. CASANOVA assumes a more erect and dignified appearance.

CASANOVA (*speaking like an actor*): Your lover deserves to be cheated on. Therefore we'll work at it all night long.

CASANOVA, satisfied with his witty remark, glances toward the hole, as if looking for applause.

MADDALENA: Come, let me take your cloak.

CASANOVA: It's impossible: it's caught on a big nail!

He laughs like an old ham. MADDALENA laughing, stretches forth her hand.

MADDALENA: Ah, rascal! What has endowed you with this nail?

CASANOVA (*chivalrous*): It's the sight of your beautiful body, my love!

The scene which follows is almost acrobatic, as in a circus. CASANOVA lifts MADDALENA, holding her up by her thighs and starts moving, stumbling, around the room. Then he stops and lays her down. He stretches out on the rug, rises to a sitting position and pulls MADDALENA on top of himself. CASANOVA begins to undress MADDALENA, loosening bows and unbuttoning buttons. Little by little, he reveals her bare body: her image, multiplied endlessly in the mirrors from every angle, becomes absurd and spectral. CASANOVA also gets undressed. Their amorous poses in the flickering candlelight seem like a macabre dance.

Slowly they bend, turn, opening their legs and arms in complicated and strange positions, like absurd and ritual movements from ancient and mysterious ceremonies.

From behind the little door, DE BERNIS is looking at the scene; we can see his bright eye appearing in the carved out eye of a fish painted on the door.

CASANOVA keeps stubbornly at his sexual act, as if it were an everyday task: one of his habitual and insatiable activities, from which he can't escape. His wide-open eyes grow more and more fixed, glossy.

We see again the bright eye of De Bernis. The eye, though, is moving away, and in its place a mouth appears, its lips slowly moving, moist and sensual.

DE BERNIS (*O. S. speaking like a priest*): Good . . . Very good, my dear young man . . .

CASANOVA, a little bewildered by this disembodied voice, gets up, almost naked and goes close to the wall, to listen to it.

DE BERNIS (*Cont.*): I would say it was an excellent performance. Moreover, your reputation precedes you. You weren't as good when she was on top; there you lacked imagination. But on the whole it's been a very good job.
CASANOVA (*mutters*): Thank you . . .

MADDALENA, smiling, comes close to Casanova, and in an affectionate, motherly way, starts to dress him.

MADDALENA: Bravo! You made me look good!

CASANOVA hadn't expected to have to leave so suddenly, but he doesn't resist and lets MADDALENA continue dressing him. She, on the contrary, remains half-naked.

CASANOVA (*embarrassed*): Then, I . . .

MADDALENA gives him a quick kiss.

MADDALENA (*In faked tone*): I love you.
DE BERNIS (*O. S.*): Farewell, young man. I hope to get to know you one day. Count on me for your business in Paris.

CASANOVA, dressed again as Pierrot, makes a dignified, long bow towards the invisible De Bernis, and a little stunned and puzzled, heads for the exit.

EXT. THE LAGOON AT VENICE. DAWN.

A storm rages. CASANOVA can hardly steer his gondola among the waves. He is soaking with sweat and sea splashes, and his teeth are visibly chattering; he is shaking. In the lagoon we see monstrous shapes: bent poles that emerge from the water; enormous drifting tufts of grass, and logs similar to crocodiles. Everything is enveloped and swept away by the violence of the wind, while the rain creates a sort of veil.

From the distance we see flickering lights of San Marco and then we hear the lost, accelerated toll of a bell.

A bolt of lightning shatters the sky and is followed by a thunder clap as loud as a cannon shot. CASANOVA is trembling.

CASANOVA (*moans*): Ave Maria gratia plena . . . dominus tecum . . .

Meanwhile, a big and powerful gondola is coming out of the dark and pulls up beside Casanova's. A harsh and loud voice comes from the gondola:

VOICE: Giacomo Casanova!

CASANOVA looks in amazement at the PEOPLE leaning out of the gondola.

There are TWO POLICEMEN, some sad figures in black clothes, and MESSER GRANDE himself, the chief of the police.

MESSER GRANDE (*in a strong, resolute voice*): Giacomo Casanova, guilty of contempt for religion, author of heretical works, owner of evil books censured by the inquisitor's Index. I, Messer Grande, by the order of the inquisitors of Venice, am putting you under arrest, to be sent to Piombi prison!

CASANOVA, sweaty and shaking, drenched, ridiculous in his Pierrot costume.

CASANOVA (*stammers*): How? And why? Messer Grande . . . Is it really you? But why?

INT. PIOMBI PRISON IN THE DOGE'S PALACE. CASANOVA'S CELL. OTHER CELLS. CORRIDORS. UNDERGROUND CELLS. ATTIC. DAY.

A cramped cell with a low ceiling. CASANOVA, half-dressed, sits on the floor. He is all sweaty from the terrible heat. He speaks to himself, or to us.

CASANOVA: The inquisitors, without any reason in the world, put me under arrest and threw me in this horrible cell at Piombi . . . For heresy, they say . . . But I'm not a heretic! I've always had faith in the holy majesty of God . . .

All at once there's a confused movement of people and things in the cell: LORENZO, the red hair jailer, and some other JAILERS are carrying a straw mattress, a chair, some food, a bottle of wine, and a couple of big books. We see the title page of one of them. It reads The Mystic City of Sister Mary of Jesus. *In illustrations of the book there is a nun tormented by the devils, a damned soul screaming in the flames, a martyr whose eyes are being pulled out.*

CASANOVA (*V. O.*): What I read was the kind of thing an eccentric mind can give birth to, the imaginings of a Spanish virgin, a melancholy fanatic . . . She said that at the age of three she used to sweep her house with the help of three hundred angels . . . sent from God . . .

While Casanova's voice is heard, we see a mixture of images of the prison: cells, where ragged, HALF-DRESSED MEN are locked up, one seated on a chamber pot; cramped corridors, where JAILERS patrol armed with bows and arrows; the underground cells, called "wells", where there's half a meter of water on the floor so that the prisoners have to crowd onto small platforms. We see the attic where huge RATS slowly move about.

CASANOVA (V. O.): As I thought of my confined, mortified youth, an immense sorrow would bewilder my soul . . . I recalled my past free life, the pleasant parties . . .

EXT. CANALS OF VENICE. DAY (RECOLLECTION).

CASANOVA and RIGHELLINI, a middle-aged man, are on a gondola slowly floating along a canal.

CASANOVA (V. O.): One day with doctor Righellini, I went to see the rooms where I meant to receive my beloved Barberina, who was my lover in that period . . .

INT. DRESSMAKER'S SHOP. DAY.

In the shop, which is a part of the living quarters, there are piles of dress materials, brocades, embroideries, as well as some dummies that here and there lift their heads, which are bald or adorned with wigs.

THE MISTRESS, old, fat, and almost bald, welcomes CASANOVA and RIGHELLINI, showing her house while making sweeping gestures. CASANOVA is quite impressive with the tricorne, wig, fashionable stockings, and small sword. He is suddenly attracted by a kind of dummy, which is not a dummy at all, but a GIRL standing still, white as wax, and keeping her eyes closed. CASANOVA, spellbound, comes closer to her.

CASANOVA: Oh, what a beautiful statue. But the artist should have colored her.

TWO GIRLS, sisters of the pale girl, burst out laughing sarcastically.

The pale girl, ANNAMARIA, opens her eyes and smiles.

Her mother, the old MISTRESS, sighs, looking troubled. Doctor RIGHELLINI touches and strokes the girl as if she were a real statue. ANNAMARIA closes her eyes again, absorbed in her own distant world.

INT. DRESSMAKER'S SHOP. BARBERINA'S ROOM. EVENING.

CASANOVA is playing with BARBERINA, a girl of fifteen or sixteen. She is huge like a giant doll, very fat, and as round as a ball; her breasts bursting out of her dress. BARBERINA laughs, and gives CASANOVA playful pushes, causing him to fall. She makes funny faces and sticks her tongue out at him, but when he gets closer to her she pulls it back in, and so on. She's like an inflated child, an erotic toy made of rubber.

ANNAMARIA'S SISTERS are at the table. They keep bringing more and more plates full of food. BARBERINA stuffs herself with a wild greed, gulps huge mouthfuls, pours down her throat great glasses of wine that run down her chin. CASANOVA regards her with satisfaction and laughs like a father happy about his daughter's appetite.

CASANOVA: Oh! Barberina my love, my little spouse, daughter, and sister! You are as big as the sea and the earth. You are the earth: a boundless landscape. Let me kiss your mountains, your lakes, your hills ...

CASANOVA gets close to her to give her a kiss, but BARBERINA bites him.

CASANOVA: Ow!

She laughs, and grabs him like a puppet, drawing him to her breast and smothering him with kisses. She also feeds him, thrusting into his mouth pieces of meat and cheese. Both laugh. ANNAMARIA SISTER'S are looking at them and also laughing. BARBERINA gets up and, with an inspired air, releases a long, harmonious fart.

INT. DRESSMAKER'S SHOP. BARBERINA'S ROOM. NIGHT.

CASANOVA and BARBERINA are in bed in the alcove. BARBERINA is on top, smothering him with kisses and attentions: she is restless and keeps shifting her enormous bottom.

BARBERINA: More, my child! More! Come on, my little one!

CASANOVA has tears of happiness in his eyes, feeling so cuddled and possessed, so perfectly enclosed in a feminine, motherly body. His movements are frenetic and full of anxiety. He touches, squeezes, kisses, caresses.

CASANOVA: You're all sweaty, my Barberina ... You seep drops as a tree drips its sap ... You are generous in this ... Look how you are losing even your lifeblood ... And your saliva too ... You are moist, dewy ... You ooze from every part, you're wet ... I'm immersed in your fluid!

EXT. DRESSMAKER'S SHOP. SMALL COURTYARD. NIGHT.

The courtyard next to Casanova's room looks like the cloister of a convent. It is small, with a well in the center. The moon lights up tufts of grass, ivy, and puddles of water among the paving stones. There is a sense of mystery in the air.

CASANOVA appears at the French door of his room and looks around. After the frenetic and sensual joy he's just had, he looks expressionless.

There is someone in the courtyard. It is the pale girl ANNAMARIA. CASANOVA comes closer to her, curious but also scared.

CASANOVA: What are you doing here?

ANNAMARIA smiles lightly.

ANNAMARIA: I'm breathing. I'm taking in a breath of sea air.
CASANOVA: Like that? In the dark?
ANNAMARIA: Always. Or else the mosquitoes will come.

CASANOVA brushes against the girl with delicacy and desire.

CASANOVA: You scared me. You look like the embodiment of the moon itself.

CASANOVA is startled, he's just seen a ship's figurehead: a mermaid atop a small column, but it's missing its arms.

CASANOVA: What is it?

ANNAMARIA: The sea brought it here. It must belong to a sunken ship. Those poor men.

CASANOVA gently draws the girl to him. She yields to him smiling, but suddenly opens her eyes wide and faints. He holds her in his arms and calls for help:

CASANOVA: Hey! Is anyone there! She fainted! The girl fainted! Quickly! A doctor!

Some windows fly open, we hear voices and footsteps come running. The shadow of a gondola, approaching as fast as a shark, stands out against the sky like a fantastic apparition.

Doctor RIGHELLINI comes ashore, runs through the courtyard toward the fainted girl. Meanwhile, some PEOPLE have arrived. They hold lanterns that light up ANNAMARIA'S body.

RIGHELLINI, with two rapid strokes of his scalpel—zip zip—lances ANNAMARIA's vein and collects her blood in a basin he has brought with him.

INT. DRESSMAKER'S SHOP. HALL. DAY.

An old MUSIC TEACHER, small, with glasses, bald and demonic, is playing a flute: a fast and melancholy arietta. ANNAMARIA, like a butterfly which has just come out of its cocoon, hesitant and staggering, is trying to follow the music, dancing with small steps. The MUSIC TEACHER is going about the room playing, while ANNAMARIA follows him, dancing.

CASANOVA enters and watches the scene, entranced. The MUSIC TEACHER, without stopping playing, beckons to him as if to invite him to join the girl. And CASANOVA, with a surge, throws himself into the dance, dancing a minuet with the apathetic ANNAMARIA. The MUSIC TEACHER sneers, satisfied. His glasses flash in the lights.

The minuet is getting more and more whirling, until ANNAMARIA and CASANOVA let themselves collapse onto a settee.

The MUSIC TEACHER disappears. CASANOVA gently caresses the wan cheeks of the girl.

CASANOVA: I sent Barberina away; I was afraid that in her greed she would eat me too!

ANNAMARIA smiles spitefully.

ANNAMARIA: And aren't you afraid of me?
CASANOVA: Perhaps, but I can't help it. I'm in love with you now. Your incorporeal beauty attracts the artist in me. I'd like to mold you . . . as a real statue of wax . . .

CASANOVA stands in front of the girl, drawing in the air with the gestures of a sculptor.

CASANOVA: I would be your Pygmalion, and like Pygmalion I'd give life to my creature . . . with my blood . . .

Suddenly ANNAMARIA has a sorrowful expression.

ANNAMARIA (*stammering*): I'm cold . . .

And she faints again.

CASANOVA lays her properly on the settee, and stands watching her, attracted by that funereal vision. He listens carefully: no one is coming. He goes to the door and closes it with care. Returning to ANNAMARIA, he kneels beside her. Then, he slowly lifts her skirt, and in sacrilegious anxiety, reaches out to touch her genitals. At that very moment, the door flings open and doctor RIGHELLINI enters running. He immediately performs a bloodletting on the girl's arm.

EXT. DRESSMAKER'S SHOP. COURTYARD. NIGHT.

The small courtyard full of weeds and puddles is magically lit up by the moon.

CASANOVA (*V. O.*): That night, I still hoped that doctor Righellini wouldn't arrive in time to keep me from my ultimate pleasure. My girl was there; as usual, she was breathing the sea air, always in the dark, to avoid the mosquitoes that are particularly fierce during that season in Venice.

ANNAMARIA is slowly walking in the courtyard; CASANOVA is spying on her, then he moves closer to her, cautiously as a cat, and jumps on her, seizing her. She gives a timid cry and faints into his arms. He smiles, pleased, lays the girl on the ground, resting her head on a tuft of grass that pops out between the stones. He looks around, sees no one. Little by little he undresses her, stroking and caressing.

CASANOVA (*mutters*): Cold as marble . . .

Anxiously, brutally, CASANOVA takes her. ANNAMARIA opens her eyes wide, utters a little scream, and clings to his body with desperate pleasure.

INT. DRESSMAKER'S SHOP. ANNAMARIA'S ROOM. NIGHT.

CASANOVA and ANNAMARIA make love on the settee in the small room; he moves with rhythmic mechanical indifference, his face devoid of pleasure, as if his mind were somewhere else . . .

A series of short mixed images follow:

CASANOVA and ANNAMARIA make love in a black gondola; at a place in the lagoon where puny drenched trees rise from the water; in Casanova's room.

CASANOVA (*V. O.*): Annamaria had regained her strength: every day I would nourish her with my passion and my blood . . . She turned into a blooming and beautiful girl. She was eager, full of the love of life. Where once there was death I had brought life.

While they are making love, Annamaria's face changes; it shows a sudden, queer curiosity. In a mischievous tone, as if she were asking him to let her in on a risqué secret, she asks:

ANNAMARIA: But tell me Giacomo! Tell me more how you escaped from Piombi prison?

INT. THE DOGE'S PALACE. HALLS, CORRIDORS, STAIRCASES, AND ENTRANCE DOOR. NIGHT.

CASANOVA and his cell-mate, a dissolute monk, MARTIN BALBI, are moving around dark halls and corridors of the palace. They've just escaped from their prison cell in the attic. They go down a wide staircase, more and more delighted.

CASANOVA (V. O.): My escape was a masterpiece of intelligence, of intuition, of planning, of timing, of patience, and of courage—qualities, all of them, bestowed on me by fortune . . .

CASANOVA and MARTIN BALBI are in front of one of the entrance doors. They don't know how to open it. As a miracle, a limping CONCIERGE appears, with a bunch of keys in his hand. In the flickering candlelight he takes the two for guests who have lost their way in the palace.

CONCIERGE: Here I am, here I am . . . I didn't know Your Lordships were still in the palace . . .

The CONCIERGE opens the door and bows.

CONCIERGE: Good night, your Lordships!

The two leave with a slight nod.

INT. MADAM D'URFÉ'S HOUSE IN PARIS. DINING ROOM. NIGHT.

The room is full of pendulum clocks and paintings with disturbing faces, staring at the OBSERVERS.

CASANOVA (V. O.): And I succeeded in reaching France.

There is a sumptuously set table, where many people are seated. MADAME D'URFÉ, an old woman, tall, imposing, has a vague, absent smile on her painted, wizened face. Among the others, there is CASANOVA and the COUNT OF SAINT-GERMAIN, a young man, with cunning eyes and a mobile face which shows faint smiles full of insinuation, then sudden severity: he gesticulates like a charlatan Frenchman.

Each of the guests has some eccentricity or other. There's an OLD KNIGHT who is absent-minded and vain, his face is painted, he has ivory dentures, his hair is lacquered with amber and he wears a small bunch of flowers at his buttonhole; a LADY getting on in years, with a very long nose, and long ears from which long earrings hang, and a long chin; a GENTLEMAN perfectly round, and red, who is constantly laughing; a FRIAR, young, with a big and threatening glass eye; a BEAUTIFUL GIRL, motionless, who is neither eating nor speaking.

CASANOVA: Now that I am guest of your beautiful country, in Paris that I already adore even though I don't know it yet, I feel safe from any trap of the vile inquisitors of Venice.
OLD KNIGHT: Oh, my dear man, you shouldn't speak ill of your homeland when you are in foreign parts.

CASANOVA blushes.

CASANOVA: Never would I speak ill of Venice! I oppose its government, which is hostile to the principles of liberty.
SAINT-GERMAIN: The world's history has always been a swing between tyranny and liberty. I've witnessed many of these changes during my life, since, as you all know, I am three hundred years old.

No one comments on, or laughs at this remark. CASANOVA bends toward the OLD KNIGHT.

CASANOVA (*in a low voice*): Who is that eccentric man?
OLD KNIGHT: The Count of Saint-Germain, the famous Initiate ...
SAINT-GERMAIN: As everyone also knows, I'm the only one who possesses the universal panacea; and do you know who gave it to me two hundred and fifty years ago? The great Leonardo da Vinci in person, who, among his researches in engineering, strategy, and anatomy, also cultivated the art of alchemy in his laboratory where, moreover, on occasion during nights of sorcerous inspiration, he painted what I regard to be his best paintings, which, unfortunately, were lost. They were portraits of devils of the first and second category—Belial,

Astarte, Lucifer, Lucifugo, with whom he had nocturnal intercourse, and who sometimes led his hand while he was painting a particularly hard drapery or landscape . . .

CASANOVA gets indignant about such a great impostor.

CASANOVA: May I ask you a question, illustrious sir? It is well known that the great Leonardo mainly painted pictures of religious subjects. Now, how could your devils help him to create the drapery of the Virgin's dress or the landscape of Golgotha?
SAINT-GERMAIN (*laughing*): And do you really believe in Leonardo's religious inspiration? He concealed the sin in his paintings. His women, even the Madonna and the Saints, were no one but young men disguised as women, young men with whom Leonardo had carnal intercourse . . .
CASANOVA (*ironic*): I imagine that Leonardo in person told you that . . . Or perhaps you also had intercourse with some of those disguised young men?

One of the guests, the FRIAR, suddenly rolls his eyes, and puts his hands on his heart.

FRIAR (*in a spectral voice*): I have come into contact with the Queen of Sheba.

MADAME D'URFÉ claps her hands like a child.

D'URFÉ: Oh, good!
FRIAR: What is a wooden well, an iron bucket, which draws stones and lets the water flow? He answered: The pot made of antimony.

SAINT-GERMAIN is eager to explain what it is all about.

SAINT-GERMAIN: Solomon's riddles. And his answer to the Queen.

Everything in CASANOVA shows his ironic skepticism.

CASANOVA: But do you really believe in this astral contact? Why then, doesn't he enter into the soul of the Queen of Sheba?

The FRIAR all of a sudden becomes clear, harsh, and firm.

FRIAR: The Queen of Sheba doesn't have a soul. Like all women.

CASANOVA: Come now, the Council of Trent dispelled that nonsense!

MADAME D'URFÉ is laughing, and with complicity takes Giacomo's hand.

FRIAR: Women only have two types of soul, men have three. Women are lacking the noble soul; that is, the nontransient one.

CASANOVA shrugs his shoulders.

CASANOVA: For a beautiful woman, even one soul is more than enough. A soul able to merge with that of a man . . . in unison with the bodies' fusion . . .

INT. MADAME D'URFÉ'S HOUSE. BEDROOM. NIGHT.

MADAME D'URFÉ guides CASANOVA pointing here and there, taking in her hands strange objects which clutter the room.

CASANOVA (V. O.): The famous Madame d'Urfé . . . an extraordinary woman . . . a great expert in necromancy.

She goes to the bookcase. She walks majestically, even though she is wearing a childlike frock, and a very tall wig made of ribbons and frills. Her face and breast are covered with powder, as if she were blanketed with dust like her books. A big magnet hangs from her neck.

D'URFÉ: This is the library that belonged to the great D'Urfé and to his wife Renata of Savoia . . . I have enriched it quite a lot. I paid one hundred thousand francs for this manuscript!

CASANOVA examines the manuscript that the woman hands him. We see it very closely—numerous sheets collected inside a red binding. The handwriting is strange, it winds in a spiral, the words form arabesques.

D'URFÉ (cont.): It is by the divine Paracelsus. My favorite! Do you know that he was neither a man nor a woman? But he wasn't, to be sure, a hermaphrodite.

Now she shows a statue of a negro, being killed by an arrow.

D'URFÉ (*cont.*): And this is the custodian of my realm: the last Bonitu', the race who inherited Atlantis.

In a corner of the room, there is a small alchemist's laboratory, with a tub full of sand, and bottles and carboys containing greenish and turquoise blue liquids. Mysterious, bent pots, and metal jars are boiling on a stove. A black CAT is coiled near the fire to warm itself.

D'URFÉ (*cont.*): This liquid has been boiling for fifteen years. It will go on boiling for another five. It is a potion which will change every metal into gold. Tell me the truth . . .

MADAME D'URFÉ puts on a wheedling and devious expression.

D'URFÉ (*cont.*): You possess the philosopher's stone, don't you?

CASANOVA modestly denies it.

CASANOVA: But no, marquise . . . What are you saying? . . .

MADAME D'URFÉ taps him on the arm.

D'URFÉ: Come now, you can tell me . . . I know that you have the famous stone . . . And also that you can communicate with the elementary spirits. You could overthrow the kingdom of France any time you like to!
CASANOVA: I would never allow myself to do such a thing. Then you overestimate me, dear friend.

MADAME D'URFÉ takes Casanova's hands.

D'URFÉ: I beg you . . . Help me in the Great Action!
CASANOVA: The Great Action! What do you mean?
D'URFÉ: Come now! You know exactly what this is all about! (*With an inspired look*) I shall die . . . in the process of changing into a male. This male will live forever. I will be able to accomplish this deed if an initiate belonging to my pyramidal sign, couples with me. In the act of delivery, my soul will enter the new born child. I will die as a woman and will return to life as a man. Forever. And you are, without doubt the most suitable man to carry out this great action!

CASANOVA, while she is speaking, goes to the window. He is thinking. Then he goes back to her. His eyes are moist with tears because of the pain and emotion stirred up by the crazy old woman. MADAME D'URFÉ, almost touched, takes his hands with affection.

D'URFÉ: But you are crying, my friend! Why?
CASANOVA: It is nothing. Show me again your treasures.

MADAME D'URFÉ takes a case, like a small coffer which is full of golden coins and shows it to him.

D'URFÉ: Here is my treasure, you will have it when you have accomplished the Great Action!

CASANOVA gets upset at the sight of the gold.

CASANOVA: I didn't mean material treasures ... but spiritual ones ... The treasures of your unearthly knowledge ...

MADAME D'URFÉ caresses CASANOVA's cheek with tenderness.

D'URFÉ: Oh my beloved ... my divine Anael has already shown me your portrait in a dream ...

EXT. MADAME D'URFÉS GARDEN. NIGHT.

CASANOVA is leaving Madame d'Urfé's house. She sees him out. Her carriage is approaching. She makes a gesture to invite CASANOVA to take a seat, implying that the carriage is now his. CASANOVA, surprised and happy, at first declines and then takes the seat; the carriage leaves. MADAME D'URFÉ waves her hand to him in a maternal and benedictory way.

EXT./INT. PARIS'S STREETS. MOVING CARRIAGE. NIGHT.

Inside the carriage, CASANOVA is happy and almost inebriated, probably thinking of the strange luck that has happened to him.

CASANOVA (V. O.): I understood that that woman was completely crazy, but I felt I had to comply with her divine madness ... And Paris seemed so beautiful, full of life and pleasures, where a thousand opportunities would be offered to the man able to catch them . . . Oh, great city of Racine and Voltaire, city of intriguing and sensual ladies . . . oh, how I loved you, how I still love you! My young heart, eager for adventures, sang a voluptuous hymn of glory within me . . .

In the dark streets we hear the sharp, nasal French typical of the slums; laughter; the rolling of other carriages. PROSTITUTES, their breasts naked, are laughing near tavern doors. A few HORSES ridden by SOL-DIERS go by dragging a clanging cannon. Suddenly Casanova's carriage skids, the HORSES swerve, the COACHMAN hurls violent insults: the carriage was about to run over someone. CASANOVA leans out the window and sees the mortified ABBOT, who provoked the accident.

He is stocky, sad, dismal with a humiliated face full of rancor. It is Casanova's brother. He suddenly recognizes CASANOVA.

ABBOT: Giacomo!

CASANOVA draws back, almost disgusted.

CASANOVA: What are you doing here?

The ABBOT tries to hug him, but CASANOVA turns him away.

ABBOT: My dear brother, I am desperate! You've got to help me; you must speak to the wicked woman who made me betray my priesthood . . . Heaven sent you! Please, dear boy, please! . . .

The ABBOT gets into his brother's carriage. CASANOVA welcomes him unwillingly, still disgusted.

ABBOT: Her name is Marcolina . . . A girl of rare beauty . . . and very tender . . .

INT. PARISIAN HOTEL. HALL. NIGHT.

MARCOLINA, very young, tall, full of rage with wild eyes, slaps the ABBOT's face.

MARCOLINA (*with Venetian accent*): Swindler! Are you going to send me back to Venice or not? How stupid I was to listen to you. You are nothing but a pig! He told me that priests can be married! He took me all the way to Paris, saying that he had to see you, Mr. Giacomo . . . He sold all my things, even my blouses!

MARCOLINA slaps the ABBOT again; he sighs without reacting.

MARCOLINA: What are you doing? Are you crying, coward?
ABBOT: You are excommunicated. I am a priest. No one can slap a minister of God!

She gives him another box on the ear.

MARCOLINA: Here, take this one to the Pope!

The ABBOT, whining, looks at CASANOVA.

ABBOT: And you, Giacomo, my dear brother, you watch without intervening? Look how the woman who swore before the crucifix she would be my wife is treating me! Do something!

CASANOVA is perplexed for a minute, then he also slaps the ABBOT.

CASANOVA: It's what you deserve, you worm, you traitor. You lead this enchanting girl to despair. Here, take this money and get out of my way. I don't want to see you anymore.

The ABBOT grabs the money that CASANOVA is handing him.

ABBOT (*whining*): And Marcolina? Isn't Marcolina coming with me?
MARCOLINA: I don't want to see you any longer, if I ever get my hands on you again, I'll . . .

MARCOLINA is about to slap him again, but he jumps away and disappears with a scream.

INT. PARISIAN HOTEL. CASANOVA'S ROOM. NIGHT.

CASANOVA, alone with MARCOLINA, assumes a paternal tone.

CASANOVA: You, my girl, are a little devil. You make my stupid fool brother lose his head over you, and suddenly you turn your back on him. He is an idiot to have fallen in love with you.

MARCOLINA: He is a presumptuous fool.

All of a sudden she becomes humble, and grabs his hand kissing it.

MARCOLINA (*whining*): Oh, Mr. Giacomo, you are so good; you can help me to go back home to my mother, to Venice.

CASANOVA impulsively clasps her in his arms; he is a bit melodramatic.

CASANOVA: I love you, and if you don't consent to become my lover I shall die.

The dialogue becomes like a puppet show: unreal with rapid thrusts and parries.

MARCOLINA: Never, since I will fall in love with you, and then when you leave me I shall die too.

CASANOVA: I'll never leave you. I just need you for an intrigue with another woman.

MARCOLINA: An intrigue? Wouldn't it be risky? I wouldn't want to get beat up.

CASANOVA: Certainly not, my heart! God, you are so beautiful! That imbecile brother of mine has good taste!

From outside, someone is knocking at the door and the whiny voice of the ABBOT is heard.

ABBOT (*O. S.*): Open, Giacomo, beloved brother! Open, Marcolina! It's very cold out here, everything is closed!

CASANOVA and MARCOLINA look at each other and burst out laughing, then they sensually kiss.

ABBOT (*O. S.*): I'm almost frozen! What are you doing in there? Oh Marcolina, I beg you, don't betray me again! Open! Open the door, Giacomo!

CASANOVA and MARCOLINA jump in bed and make love frenetically. Outside, the ABBOT keeps knocking.

INT. PARISIAN HOTEL. CASANOVA'S ROOM. DAWN.

CASANOVA, almost naked, is sleeping soundly. He is lying on Marcolina's naked body. MARCOLINA is also sleeping.

INT. MADAME D'URFÉ'S HOUSE. BEDROOM. LABORATORY. NIGHT.

A small room, narrow but with very high ceilings. There are many reddish lights, images, relics, and magic things neatly arranged: everything is disturbing, queer, and dreadful. In a corner there is a small tub, deep and narrow.

MADAME D'URFÉ stands in the middle of the room.

D'URFÉ (*solemnly*): I am ready. The hour of Venus has come.

Slowly she begins to get undressed. It is a long ceremony, since the woman wears many clothes, which fall little by little, one after another; every time it seems to be finished, there is always another petticoat, or vest, or panties. CASANOVA, worried, is watching that frightening striptease.

Now, MADAME D'URFÉ is naked; her breasts sag and her flesh is flabby. She stretches her hands out toward him.

D'URFÉ: Take me. Let the Great Action be fulfilled.
CASANOVA: Yes. One moment . . . We are still in the hour of Mars . . .

A pendulum clock strikes twice. MARCOLINA enters, dressed up like a small red and black devil. She gives a sheet to MADAME D'URFÉ.

MARCOLINA: What is written on water, only in water can be read.

MADAME D'URFÉ, astonished, looks at the sheet, which is white. Then her face brightens.

D'URFÉ: I understand everything!

She dips the sheet in the tub water. These words appear on the sheet: "I am dumb, but not deaf. I come out of the Rhone to take a bath. The time of Oromasis has come."

MARCOLINA gives out a scream full of joy, a little shrill, then she rapidly gets undressed, and whispering quick words in Venetian helps MADAME D'URFÉ to get into the tub. She washes MADAME D'URFÉ, stroking her, caressing her, kissing her with genuine, incredibly sensual pleasure, as if she were truly attracted by that flabby body, as if the old lady were her beloved doll.

MADAME D'URFÉ is amazed and delighted. She also starts stroking the girl. MARCOLINA kisses her with affection on her breast, on her belly and even on her groin. The old woman moans with pleasure. CASANOVA is watching enchanted, then he too gets undressed. Now suddenly, they are all together in bed; he breathes heavily, sweats, while MARCOLINA wipes his forehead.

CASANOVA (*V. O.*): The thunderbolt was there—I had it, but not enough force to make it explode ... Since I couldn't bear the battle any longer, I decided to fake it, improvising an action full of convulsions that ended in stillness.

CASANOVA pretends to enjoy the pleasures of the old woman, then falls down as though dead.

INT. MOVING CARRIAGE. NIGHT.

CASANOVA is lying in a small cramped carriage made of black wood; nodding, he every now and then takes a big swallow out of a bottle of wine he keeps in his hand. Near him there is Madame d'Urfé's box full of gold coins.

CASANOVA (*in a low voice*): Certainly that gold was a help, but it wasn't the only reason ... I have always believed in the occult sciences. Without Marcolina's help I would never have been able to possess the old lady ... a handsome woman, of course ... with class ... clean, too ... but then her flesh was rather withered! But I have always loved the game to be chewy! (*he laughs wearily*)... You shouldn't judge me for what I am not. I suffer the consequences of what I do. Women give, and take ... Oh, I know that very well ... (*yawning*) All my life has been ...

(*he yawns again*) If I have had happiness, I've also had a lot of grief: joy and sorrow counterbalance each other, as do good and bad . . .

CASANOVA takes a gulp of wine, his head is drooping and his jaw drops in an idiotic grimacing smile as the carriage continues its shaky run.

EXT./INT. CARRIAGE. INN FORLÍ. NIGHT.

The carriage stops in front of an inn. We catch a glimpse of its sign.

The COACHMAN shakes CASANOVA to wake him up. Automatically, like a puppet, he gets out and enters the inn.

INT. INN FORLÍ. BEDROOM. DAY.

A bedroom is full of PEOPLE who are shouting all together: there is an old man, a CAPTAIN, in bed, wearing a night cap, screaming sentences in Latin; a GROUP OF POLICEMEN, with rifles and carrying over their shoulder bows and arrows, who hurl sharp orders in Italian; an INNKEEPER who is speaking first to the man in bed, then to the POLICEMEN, also in Italian.

CASANOVA dominates every one by his height, and he is speaking first to the man in Latin, then to the POLICEMEN in Italian, then to the INNKEEPER, also in Italian. After a little while, CASANOVA bends over, grabs a saber that is leaning against a chair, and lifts it up.

CASANOVA (*screaming*): He is Hungarian! Look at this! He is a Hungarian officer! You are committing a crime!
INNKEEPER: I had to unlock the door myself.
CASANOVA: You are a burglar! All of you leave or I'll report you to your superiors!

The POLICEMEN laugh. CASANOVA turns to the CAPTAIN and speaks to him in Latin. Then he takes some documents that lie rolled up on the table, spreads them out in front of the POLICEMAN, and with broad gestures invites them to leave. The POLICEMEN leave, the INNKEEPER remains.

INNKEEPER: Sir, I beg you, let's not make a fuss in my inn!

CASANOVA slaps him.

CASANOVA: Rascal!

The INNKEEPER leaves, humiliated.

The CAPTAIN bursts out laughing.

CAPTAIN: What a strange law! All this fuss because they understood that I was in bed with a woman!

From the sheets, a smiling fresh face of a WOMAN with short uncombed hair like a boy's pops out. They all laugh.

CASANOVA: Are you Hungarian too?
HENRIETTE: I am French. My name is Henriette.
CASANOVA: In which language do you speak with your lover, then?
HENRIETTE: We never speak to each other. For what we do together, it's not necessary to speak!

She slides again under the sheets. The CAPTAIN joins her. The two bodies toss about. CASANOVA, curious, lifts the sheet and looks. The atmosphere is now full of joy, laughter, playful remarks. The INNKEEPER comes back bringing a tray, as if nothing had happened.

INNKEEPER: Coffee, gentlemen!

INT./EXT. CARRIAGE. MOUNTAINS. DAY.

A carriage is clambering with difficulty up an Apennine road. Inside, the CAPTAIN is seated on a foldaway seat. On the rear seat there is CASANOVA who holds HENRIETTE in between his open legs. He wears elegant traveling clothes, the other two wear military uniforms, red jacket, braiding, bandoleers, black shining boots. HENRIETTE has a smiling, light presence.

Out of the windows there is a grand perspective of leafy branches. They create changing shadows inside the carriage.

HENRIETTE (*to Casanova*): But you must be uncomfortable, with my weight on your legs.

CASANOVA: On the contrary! It is a truly pleasant honor. I am sorry the journey is going to be so short.

HENRIETTE laughs. The CAPTAIN looks at them frowning, not understanding. CASANOVA translates the sentence into Latin. The CAPTAIN gives a faint smile.

The carriage stops in an oak wood, up in the mountains. Many trees lie on the ground, evidently cut down recently. There is also a big stack of stripped logs.

CASANOVA and the CAPTAIN are seated on a log eating. All around them, there is a large quantity of food: baskets and plates with different kinds of meat, fishes, pies, cured pork meats, and so forth, and a lot of bottles of wine. The two are cheerfully eating and speaking in Latin. But CASANOVA is often turning his eyes on HENRIETTE who, instead of eating, is running among the oaks. She suddenly stops, disappears behind the stack, then runs out again. Using a hatchet she has just found, she cuts down a small tree.

CASANOVA (*V.O.*): But who is this girl? She combines a fine sensitivity with the appearance of utter dissoluteness. In Parma, she says she'll take her leave. Goodbye to my hope. But who is she then? Has she a husband in Parma, or is she sure she will find her lover there? Or she's in search of unbridled liberty . . .

The CAPTAIN suddenly intervenes, as if he had heard Casanova's thoughts.

CAPTAIN: No, it isn't like that, even though I have to admit that I don't know who this beautiful and mysterious woman is. She asked me for help and protection. I granted it to her and became by chance her fortuitous companion. But I would be infinitely happy to leave Henriette in your hands.

The CAPTAIN has tears in his eyes. CASANOVA too, is moved and hugs him impetuously.

EXT. THE STREETS OF PARMA. DAY

Clean, cobbled streets, a few carriages go by, there is a certain atmosphere of military occupation—in Parma both the French and the Spanish are competing for influence.

A group of BEAUTIFUL LADIES and ELEGANT GENTLEMEN go by, laughing and making facetious remarks in French. A group of SPANISH MEN stride along, speaking with solemnity; passing in front of a church, they all make the sign of the cross.

CASANOVA is walking, looking all around; being near the Spanish, he also crosses himself. He comes close to a store. In its window fabrics, linen, lingerie are displayed. The OWNER, a fat and spiteful woman, sits watching people out for a stroll.

INT. STORE. DAY

CASANOVA enters the store, looks around and approaches the OWNER.

CASANOVA: Madam, I would like to buy some lingerie.

OWNER: I'll send for someone who can speak French, sir.

CASANOVA: But I am Italian!

OWNER: Oh! It's very rare today. Don Filippo has arrived, and Madam French[*] is on her way.

CASANOVA: Good, good! Money will flow!

OWNER: Maybe, but it is difficult to get use to these new habits. It's a mixture of French licentiousness and Spanish jealousy which make us dizzy. What can I do for you today?

CASANOVA: Some fine cloth for twenty-four blouses, cotton for petti-coats, corsets, bonnets, muslin and handkerchiefs. We also need to find good dress-makers who work quickly, because the lady needs every-thing. She is practically naked. By the way, do you have Paris gloves?

OWNER: Most delicate ones. My daughter will help you try them on. (*Calling*) Fiorenza, bring the silk caps!

[*]The French Princess, Louise Elizabeth, and her husband, the Spanish Duke Philip, received the duchies of Parma in the middle of the eighteenth century.

FIORENZA, a thin girl, sniffling from a cold, brings a package of silk condoms in different colors and cuts. CASANOVA chooses the condoms: some of them have strings to attach them, others have ornaments and fringe: in short, they are condoms of the 18th century.

CASANOVA: These look appropriate . . . Would you help me to try one on, dear?

FIORENZA, still sniffling and with a surly air, unbuttons Casanova's fly.

INT. HOTEL IN PARMA. DAY.

Standing erect in the middle of a hotel room is HENRIETTE. Finally dressed as a woman, she is beautiful, with a powdered wig, a stupendous low-necked dress and makeup. She has a new expression. More pensive and almost melancholic. But she is also undoubtedly very pleased with herself. She has undergone a transformation like that of Pinocchio: from an irresponsible rascal into a living creature. CASANOVA, bewitched, looks at her incomparable beauty with respect. He is breathing hard, and at a loss for words.

The CAPTAIN, by himself, looks on, sadly sneering. He shakes his head, muttering a few sentences in Latin before leaving. CASANOVA takes a step forward, and humbly and passionately kisses HENRIETTE's white hand. She sighs and smiles faintly, looking at the window.

HENRIETTE (*whispers*): Am I no longer the same person?
CASANOVA: No, no. You are no longer the bold and quaint officer that I met . . .

From outside the window the sound of violins and violas is coming: a small serenade accompanied by a voice that sings in French.

HENRIETTE: But I am the same Henriette who has committed three follies in her life.

The serenade stops. We hear someone screaming angrily in Spanish. Two shots follow. HENRIETTE paying no attention to the sounds coming from outside, utters with theatrical solemnity:

HENRIETTE: The last, wonderful folly, was meeting you.

CASANOVA kneels down in front of her. HENRIETTE looks like an 18th century statuette. She slowly bends over him till she can kiss his mouth.

INT. SALON OF DU BOIS'S COUNTRY HOUSE. STAGE. NIGHT.

A spacious vaulted room. In armchairs, set in concentric semicircles, the GUESTS are seated, for the most part French and Spanish. In a corner, a NEGRO holding a chandelier stands still like a Tiepolo painting.

CASANOVA (*V. O.*): We were invited to a concert in the house of the hunchback Du Bois. A very intelligent man.

Six or seven ACTORS dressed up as ancient Romans crowd the small stage. They are singing in a very loud voice, accompanied by string instruments. Among them are a couple of CASTRATI, dressed as women, but easily recognizable.

The GUESTS enjoy the powerful, almost menacing music, and in the meantime they talk to each other without lowering their voices.

GUESTS : Good passage ... The soprano could sing contralto ... Ah! That was a sour note!

At the end of the performance, the GUESTS applaud, while the SER-VANTS are bringing sorbets in big wine glasses. The sorbets are served to the music of a cello solo. CASANOVA, in the most elegant black suit, and HENRIETTE are among the guests. She seems troubled; every now and then she glances around and behind her.

CASANOVA: Don't be anxious, my darling. Don't deny yourself the pleasure of this divine music.
HENRIETTE: I am not. And then, I am sure that Du Bois doesn't know anyone who is eager to meet me.

The cello solo is finished. While the CELLIST is thanking the audience, HENRIETTE gets up and goes close to him.

HENRIETTE: Your fingers have been wonderful. And your instrument, also ... How beautiful it is!

She caresses the cello as if it were a lover and she smiles sweetly.

HENRIETTE (*whispers*): I'll try to draw something out of it too.

HENRIETTE starts playing the cello. She plays very well: a delicate and longing music. They all, full of admiration, fall silent. .

CASANOVA stares in amazement at her: the unexpected performance fascinates and almost frightens him.

No sooner has HENRIETTE finished than they all burst into a storm of cheering.

GUESTS (*crying*): Brava! Encore!

CASANOVA gets up to compliment HENRIETTE. But she strikes up again, the same piece, giving an encore.

CASANOVA, standing near the French window that opens onto the garden, gives a sob full of emotion. He leaves abruptly.

EXT. *DU BOIS'S COUNTRY HOUSE. GARDEN. NIGHT.*

CASANOVA wanders around the garden, crying. Among the trees are some telescopes of different sizes, pointing at different directions, toward the stars. They look like small cannons. CASANOVA is sobbing without restraint and also looking at the stars, like the telescopes.

CASANOVA (*to himself*): But who is she? Who is this Henriette? Who is the treasure I became the owner of? It isn't possible ... Oh stars, you tell me. Shout that I, Casanova, am the blissful mortal possessor of such a treasure ...

From inside the house, we hear the cello, which is repeating once more the same piece. Suddenly DU BOIS appears in the dark.

DU BOIS: Casanova! Where are you? ... You are weeping!

CASANOVA flings his arms round Du Bois's neck.

CASANOVA: Oh my dear friend! I am so happy! And I am so frightened!

DU BOIS: What an extraordinary woman! Listen! It is the sixth time she has repeated the same piece! Come! Dinner is ready!

INT. DU BOIS'S COUNTRY HOUSE. DINING-ROOM. NIGHT.

The GUESTS are seated around the table, on high, bulky, very uncomfortable armchairs. The portions are enormous: every dish is full of fowl, chops, and sausages. The SERVANTS bring a tray full of boiled potatoes still in their skin.

DU BOIS (*pointing at the tray*): This is something novel and good. It's a present Mr. Parmentier sent me from Paris. Potatoes!

CASANOVA tastes a potato.

CASANOVA: Delicious . . . They are the fruits of a new tree, very short, an apple of the earth.

A SPANIARD, severe and frowning, turns to HENRIETTE.

SPANIARD: Can you play other instruments besides the cello?
HENRIETTE: No, only that one. I learnt when I was in convent. Had it not been for the explicit order of the bishop, the Mother Superior wouldn't have allowed me to play.
SPANIARD: And why?
HENRIETTE (*with delightful irony*): That pious bride of Christ thought that, holding the cello, I assumed an indecent pose . . .

All the FRENCH burst out of laughing. In contrast, the SPANISH blush, bite their lips, and bend their heads over the plates.

At that moment, a STRANGER appears at the door, we can barely see his face, because it is in shadow.

STRANGER (*in a deep voice*): I am sorry for being so late.

DU BOIS jumps to his feet:

DU BOIS: But, come in, make yourself comfortable, Mr. D'Antoine!

HENRIETTE sees the newcomer and turns pale.

HENRIETTE (*mutters to herself*): D'Antoine . . .

CASANOVA glances at her with anxiety and despair.

INT. HOTEL IN PARMA. CASANOVA'S BEDROOM. NIGHT.

The room is lit up by the flame of a porcelain stove, which is solemn as a monument. On a high bed which rests on four long and thin iron legs CASANOVA and HENRIETTE give themselves up to a night of passionate love. The jerks of the two bodies, which we see indistinctly under the sheets, give the idea of a wild, young, irresistible passion.

CASANOVA: . . . for ever . . . for ever with you, my love . . . Oh, you cruel Henriette! You all but kill me with your cello . . . Oh, tell me, tell me more, I implore you, what other virtues do you hide from me . . . shouldn't I die . . .

She merely laughs charmingly, and sighs, giving out cries of pleasure. Every now and then we get a glimpse of her face, bright and taken by lust, and his, contorted with pleasure and soaked with tears.

INT. HOTEL IN PARMA. CASANOVA'S BEDROOM. MORNING.

CASANOVA is tossing and turning in his sleep. Finally he opens his eyes and looks for Henriette beside him. But she is no longer there. He wakes up completely, sits up, and catches the sight of someone standing in the middle of the room. The hunchback DU BOIS, upright and stiff, gives him a short dry bow. He also smiles, with a soft malicious laugh.

DU BOIS: I apologize for entering without being announced, but the servants let me in with no hesitation.
CASANOVA: Apologies accepted, although your behavior is rather strange. To what do I owe the honor of this visit?

DU BOIS sits astride a small chair, which seems made to measure for him, and says in a quick, serious, almost businesslike tone:

DU BOIS: As you have realized, Miss Henriette is no longer here . . .
CASANOVA (*interrupting him passionately*): Where is she? What's happened to her?

DU BOIS: Nothing, my dear friend. She is fine, better off than you and I, but imperious duty has induced her to leave before dawn; I saw her briefly while she was getting into Mr. D'Antoine's carriage, and she asked me to come here to forewarn you and advise you to do nothing, absolutely nothing to trace her ...

CASANOVA: But what are you saying? Why did she have to leave? Who is D'Antoine?

DU BOIS hits CASANOVA with his stick in a gesture only apparently playful and harmless; he indeed hurts him.

DU BOIS: There you go, getting excited again! I can't say more, other than Henriette is not available: a very influential personage in a European court has complete power over her, and his emissary D'Antoine has come to bring her back to her rightful place ...

CASANOVA jumps on the bed; DU BOIS hits him again with his stick, but CASANOVA, with an involuntary shove, throws the still-seated hunchback to the floor.

CASANOVA: No matter what, I'll find her! I can't lose her, even if I must fight all the armies of Europe! Where is she? Which way did she go?

DU BOIS is on the floor, like a turtle rolled over on its back, still astride the chair and laughing brightly.

DU BOIS: Toward the mountains, of course!

CASANOVA: I shall leave immediately to find her again! And at all costs! She is my only love!

He shouts at the hotel servants:

CASANOVA: Hot water! Hot water!

DU BOIS laughs louder and louder.

INT. MOVING CARRIAGE. LONDON. NIGHT. YEARS LATER.

In the carriage, CASANOVA and TWO WOMEN are violently quarreling.

The OLD WOMAN is trying to snatch a handkerchief from the hands of Casanova, who is holding out against her, but he has to defend himself from the scratches of the YOUNG WOMAN, who is hurling herself at him like a cat.

OLD WOMAN: You thief! There were two hundred! And also the corsets! And the silver mirror.

CASANOVA: I won't tolerate these insinuations! Lord Winston in person paid for his share! (*To the young woman*) And you keep your hands off of me, you whore!

YOUNG WOMAN (*furiously*): Me, a whore? Certainly not with you, you impotent old man!

OLD WOMAN: I curse the day that I welcomed you in my house! Damn you, you and your astrology!

CASANOVA: You and your daughter be damned! I'll report you to the police! I know you poisoned my food!

YOUNG WOMAN: Ah, yes! Let's go immediately to the police! You'll repeat your accusations to them!

OLD WOMAN: First, I want everything back! The locket included!

CASANOVA: That's enough! Let me out of here before I cut both of you to bits with my sword! I swear to God that I'll kill you, witches! I will kill you!

EXT. BRIDGE AND SHORE OF THE THAMES. NIGHT.

The carriage stops on a bridge and CASANOVA gets out, or rather plunges from it, dragging with him bags and suitcases, which are quarreled over by the TWO WOMEN, who don't want to leave them to him. But in the end, with a last tug, CASANOVA takes the luggage as the carriage is leaving. The OLD WOMAN spits in his face.

Darkness; night and fog. CASANOVA is alone on the bridge, and he is desperate. He feels sorry for himself.

CASANOVA: No ... This is too much! Mortified by those two witches who have destroyed and robbed me ... Giacomo! Is your star drawing to its setting? You have born wicked insults ... and have known the most humiliating defeat of your life: for the first time your senses couldn't match your desire ... Eros is abandoning you ... gloomy Thanatos is rising!

He sobs, looking sadly at the luggage scattered at his feet.

CASANOVA: Should I appear before Death, I will go dressed in my best clothes. Fully dressed, I will enter into the ancient courts of ancient men ...

He pulls out of the suitcase a magnificent suit and a beaver tricorne and starts to put it on, stripping and shivering.

CASANOVA: I will meet Dante, Petrarca, Ariosto ... and you, Torquato Tasso! My tender friend ... whose verses come back to me now in this supreme moment ...

While CASANOVA is getting dressed, he recites Tasso's verses:

CASANOVA: O Death, O lull in every human state,
a dried-up plant I am, with sapless leaves
Alas, come, gentle Death, heed my lament;
come, tender one, and with a tender hand
cover these eyes, embrace these icy limbs.

CASANOVA, having put on the elegant clothes, is slowly going down toward the river's edge. He moves slowly forward in the cold murky water, shivering, weeping, looking around. Suddenly his attention is attracted by some shadows walking along the shore with a glare of torches. They are muttering and laughing.

CASANOVA looks more carefully and sees a GIANT WOMAN, almost an elephant. She holds the hand of a SMALL MAN, who is leading her like a beast. The GIANT WOMAN stops at the water's edge, spreads her huge legs and pees with the strength of a horse.

CASANOVA is enchanted, curious, and attracted. Without realizing what he is doing, he comes out of the water and goes toward her. But she is going up to the bridge, moving away. CASANOVA, sunk in mud and drenched, can't move quickly and loses sight of her. Yet he tries to keep following her.

EXT./INT. FAIR BOOTHS. WHALE. NIGHT.

CASANOVA, lost, moves about the booths of a fair, still looking for the GIANT WOMAN. He is followed by a SERVANT with a wheelbarrow, on which his luggage is piled.

A frightening, stuffed whale is a subject of curiosity to the FEW PEOPLE around. Two ladders are leaning against the whale, so to go inside and get out. In front of the entrance, a BARKER, wearing fanciful sailor's clothes (perhaps he holds a harpoon) is inviting people to go in; his words seem to be intended especially for Casanova.

BARKER (*in a quick rhythm*): The queen of the whales, the Leviathan of Jonah! Everyone can enter! Her womb is still warm! A female whale! And the sea, it is female as well. But, you don't dare! Don't enter, said the fox! Enter, said the wolf! . . . Women and devils travel the same road! First a kiss and then a scratch. You will never be her same height: either too tall or too short! . . . Woman, as big as the sea, with one kiss she can drown you! Come in, Sir. The whale is waiting for you.

CASANOVA has entered the whale. Against its side he is looking at a series of projections from a magic lantern. These images are odd and monstrous. We see hideous women, always endowed with strong thighs, huge buttocks, and enormous breasts.

CASANOVA shakes his head horrified, and leaves.

INT. TAVERN. NIGHT.

CASANOVA has entered in the big tavern, continually looking around for the giant woman. Suddenly someone calls him.

EDGAR: Giacomo!

CASANOVA recognizes in amazement a friend of his, EDGAR, a young man, a drug addict with an ironic demeanor. He is lying on a bench.

CASANOVA: Edgar!
EDGAR: What are you doing here, Giacomo?

CASANOVA: A strange chance has brought me here. A short time ago, tired of the thousand insults, I had decided to put an end to my life. I was about to drown myself in the Thames.

EDGAR laughs and finishes his glass.

EDGAR: Kill yourself, you? What a crazy man you are. Suicide is too beautiful a thing to toss off in such a hurry and in the cold of the river. (*Speaking to the innkeeper*) Another glass of warm wine, with ale and no sugar.
CASANOVA: Beer and red wine!
EDGAR: You should try opium. Those who take it experience the predominance of the divine over instinct . . . An untroubled serenity . . . A majestic light . . .

EDGAR points to a group of SAILORS who are taking some big, dark pills out of pot set on the counter.

EDGAR (*cont.*): Many people take it to save money. Here in England not every one can afford wine. And the opium makes you travel . . . Marvelous trips in lands which don't even exist.
CASANOVA: I also travel a lot, but in reality.
EDGAR: Yours is a trip through woman's body and doesn't lead you anyplace. But tell me: why did you back off from your decision to kill yourself?
CASANOVA: While I was already sinking in the muddy and cold water, reciting a sonnet of Tasso, I saw an extraordinary woman passing by. She was probably seven feet tall. She made me curious, and I felt that I had to follow her. But unfortunately I lost sight of her . . . and I don't think I will find her again.
EDGAR: Here she is, if I am not mistaken.

And EDGAR points at the GIANT WOMAN, who is seated at a table, arm wresting with some strong SAILORS, beating them all. CASANOVA, enchanted, gets up and goes to her. Her BARKER (the small man who accompanied her to the river) is shouting:

BARKER: The strongest woman in the world. Caught in India by our soldiers. A glass of beer to the man who can beat her! Who wants to try?

The GIANT WOMAN stops in front of the counter and opens her mouth in a sinister smile: she is missing two front teeth. CASANOVA, attracted, fingers her muscles, then keeps touching her here and there, like a horse. Afterwards, he moves back and is about to go away.

BARKER (*cont.*): The brave man will fight with the strong woman. The coward will run away.

CASANOVA turns, stung.

CASANOVA: What do you mean, sir?

The BARKER gives him a teasing bow.

BARKER: Nothing, sir. Do you think perhaps I've called you coward? A gentleman of your caliber . . . certainly European. Can he be lacking in honor?

CASANOVA raises his voice.

CASANOVA: I alone am the custodian of my honor and I consider any reference to it offensive.

The GIANT WOMAN laughs. The other PEOPLE in the tavern laugh too. The BARKER shows a surly smile.

BARKER: Then, do you agree to fight for a glass of beer?
CASANOVA (*nobly*): I don't want your beer. But I'll certainly fight. I am a Venetian gentleman. I fought against the Turks. Come now, madam.

With a chivalrous bow, CASANOVA invites the GIANT WOMAN to place her arm on the counter. Then he also positions his arm, leaning on his elbow. The competition starts, amid laughter and encouragements. CASANOVA struggles. He does his best, turning red as a turkey. The GIANT WOMAN looks at him with a pleased smile and whispers:

GIANT WOMAN (*in a Venetian accent*): What's to be done?

CASANOVA is amazed.

CASANOVA: You are also from Venice?
GIANT WOMAN: From Treviso.

CASANOVA, mortified, beseeches her:

CASANOVA: Let me beat you . . . Don't let me look like a fool . . .

But following an easy start, she beats him. The ONLOOKERS burst into loud applause. CASANOVA, deafened and discouraged, looks around.

EDGAR (*with sad irony*): Well, even this time you've lost . . .
CASANOVA (*arrogantly*): With a lady I couldn't engage thoroughly.
EDGAR: You're completely crazy.

EDGAR lies on two chairs, and without bothering about his friend any longer becomes absorbed in a drowsy and drug-induced daydream.

EXT. FAIR BOOTHS. NIGHT.

CASANOVA and the GIANT WOMAN walk slowly among the booths and the taverns near the port. She is being loving and seems almost to regret having beaten CASANOVA.

CASANOVA: But how did you end up here in London, oh, mythological creature?
GIANT WOMAN: An unhappy marriage. He sold me as if I were a beast. I didn't know how to protest.

She sighs, and smiles.

GIANT WOMAN: But I like it here. I have a good job. People are honest here, and good.

The two set out for the woman's booth.

INT. GIANT WOMAN'S BOOTH. NIGHT.

GIANT WOMAN: This is where I perform.

The room is circular. On a sort of stage, there is a big, high tangle of ropes, like an enormous web. The GIANT WOMAN describes her performance, miming it and moving around.

GIANT WOMAN: My friend invites men to fight with me ... If someone consents, he comes up here ... and I take my position in this corner ...

She climbs onto the web.

GIANT WOMAN: Then I jump down ... like that ...

She demonstrates.

GIANT WOMAN (*cont.*): And we fight. I always win. Usually, when I pin a man with his back to the ground he has an ejaculation.
CASANOVA (*amazed*): Oh?
GIANT WOMAN: Oh yes, he comes!

CASANOVA starts touching her, full of desire. She takes him to her quarters in a corner of the booth, furnished with many Venetian objects.

GIANT WOMAN: This is my home.
CASANOVA: You are an extraordinary woman ... I'm already in love with you ... I adore you ...

The GIANT WOMAN, indifferent, lifts her arms, flexes her biceps. She is tall as a statue and as unreachable. In the meantime, she's humming a Venetian popular song. CASANOVA tries to kiss her; at first she turns her face, then suddenly she seizes him and lays him on the floor. The two hug, kiss, and make love.

CASANOVA (*Sobbing*): Please! Please! Have pity!

They make love passionately.

CASANOVA: Don't leave me ... Marry me, my love!

Above his voice, we hear an indifferent, almost mocking voice of the old Casanova.

CASANOVA (*V. O.*): But I didn't marry that one either, just as I didn't marry that other time, in Turkey ...

EXT. ISMAIL EFFENDI'S GARDEN IN TURKEY. DAY.

TURKISH NOBLES, only men, are sitting on very short stools around small tables set with food.

CASANOVA is going about the magnificent garden; the GARDENER, a Neapolitan slave, is showing him around.

GARDENER: Look how beautiful these plants are! Here in Turkey the flowers are ten times bigger than ours, the earth and water are very good.
CASANOVA: You are not Turkish, I assume.
GARDENER: I am from Naples, I am a sailor, I was captured and taken here as a slave thirty years ago. But I like it here very much! I take care of the garden. Ismail Effendi is a good master, the best anyone could hope for.

The GARDENER blows a kiss toward ISMAIL, a young man with a very white complexion, somewhat plump, and with large black eyes.

The TURKS are talking to one another, moving jerkily, raising their voices, with short, shrill bursts of laughter.

CASANOVA goes back to the group; he sits, they offer him a pipe of tobacco. An old man, YUSUF, dignified, with a white beard, is smiling subtly.

YUSUF: The pleasure of tobacco is purely sensuous. The true pleasures are the ones which touch only the mind, independent of the senses.
CASANOVA: I can't image what pleasures my mind would have without the use of my senses!
YUSUF: Forty years ago I thought the same way you do. But, my son, pleasures that arouse passions upset the mind, therefore we can't call them pleasures.
CASANOVA: You surprise me. I should think you had a very unhappy youth?
YUSUF: Not at all. Always healthy and happy. But I was able to choose the great pleasures. And the great pleasures are those which don't stir passions but increase peace of the mind. Only religion can lead man to eternal salvation!

Hearing the word religion, all the GUESTS piously touch their hearts, lips and foreheads.

CASANOVA: Do you believe your religion to be the only true one?
YUSUF: I don't know if it is the only one. But certainly yours, Christianity, cannot be universal.
CASANOVA: And why not?
YUSUF: Because bread and wine are unknown in two-thirds of the world. The Koran can be followed everywhere!

A slender girl, ZELMI, with beautiful eyes, which are all we can see of her veiled face, comes to pick Yusuf up. He gets up with difficulty, and leans against her arm. CASANOVA looks on in admiration; YUSUF smiles.

YUSUF: My daughter Zelmi has come to take me home.

And he adds, speaking to CASANOVA in a soft voice:

YUSUF: She is fifteen years old, she can speak Greek and Italian, she can play the harp. She will inherit all my possessions. She does nothing, but what I say. If you become Muslim, and learn our language, religion and habits, . . . Zelmi shall be your wife!

CASANOVA is at a loss for words. YUSUF begins to leave .

YUSUF: Now that I've sown the seeds in your mind, you won't be able to think of anything else. You will follow the irrevocable decree of God. And I foresee that you will become a column of the Ottoman empire.

ISMAIL who has heard Yusuf's words, laughs, amused.

EXT. ISMAIL EFFENDI'S GARDEN. THE POOL. NIGHT.

It is getting dark, night is falling. ISMAIL and CASANOVA are alone in the garden lighted up by the moon.

CASANOVA: God's will be done. I have faith in Him. That venerable Yusuf, so wise, will be my father . . . Besides your God is very similar to ours. What do you think, Ismail, my friend?

ISMAIL: There is a lot of truth in what you say.

CASANOVA: I'll start a family down here. Zelmi will learn how to speak Venetian. The climate here is mild. Is Zelmi beautiful? Have you ever seen her face?

ISMAIL: Ah no . . . Here it is forbidden; no one would dare uncover a woman's face.

ISMAIL sighs and looks at CASANOVA gently.

ISMAIL: We love the mystery, the concealed things, the night . . . the moon and the stars are our banner.

ISMAIL looks around, and takes CASANOVA by the hand.

ISMAIL: There is something interesting . . . Come. Quietly. Two or three of my women are having a bath.

CASANOVA lights up with sensual curiosity. The two reach a pavilion from which they perceive some naked WOMEN swimming in a pool or walking on the steps behind the pool. CASANOVA looks at them, attentive and moved by the poetic vision. Beside him ISMAIL whispers in an insinuating voice:

ISMAIL: "Look at my breasts, more beautiful than a young girl's breast: my saliva is sweeter than honey . . . " Do you know *A Thousand and One Nights?*

ISMAIL, with a suggestive, imploring smile, is slowly baring his breast, which is almost like that of a young girl. CASANOVA, embarrassed, bursts out laughing. ISMAIL laughs too, but lasciviously.

ISMAIL: It is a great book, *A Thousand and One Nights* . . . "Admire the splendor of my face, my flexible neck, the delicacy of my lips . . . "

CASANOVA looks at the naked WOMEN, looks at ISMAIL, then again at the women, then at Ismail, who purses his lips and places a very light kiss on Casanova's mouth. CASANOVA finds in his arms the young man, so passive and ingratiating. And vents on him his excitement aroused by the situation: the sensuality of the surroundings, of the women bathing, and of Ismail's dark charm. While the camera frames the WOMEN or enchanted and strange corners of the garden, we hear from the pavilion Ismail's voice. He is singing his hymn of victory:

ISMAIL: "All night long he lies in my arms, cheek to cheek, a peerless beauty among human beings . . . The full moon has risen, lighting us up with her beams . . . Beg her not to denounce us to Allah!"

A bright laugh from both of them follows.

INT. ROYAL PALACE IN VIENNA. THRONE ROOM. DAY.

The ruler of Austria, MARIA TERESA, a fat woman in her mid-thirties, dressed with bonnet and shawl, more like an old maid than an empress, is seated carelessly on a throne that looks like a high-chair. She is apparently speaking to herself or to someone we don't see.

MARIA TERESA: Pride wraps itself in the flag of dignity . . . Avarice can produce useful savings . . . Anger is nothing more than an illness . . . Gluttony can be confused with a refined palate . . .

The EMPRESS licks her lips with greed.

MARIA TERESA (*cont.*): And laziness has its punishment in boredom . . . But lust!

She gazes into space with glaring eyes.

MARIA TERESA (*cont.*): Lust, no . . . I cannot forgive it! Should my subjects want to enjoy that pleasure, they shall marry!

EXT. VIENNA'S STREET. NIGHT.

The streets' cobbles are damp and slippery.

MARIA TERESA (*V. O.*): But those shall die who try to obtain it with money!

We see sharp roofs in a gothic settings. CASANOVA is walking slowly, looking around. A beautiful Arab or Turkish PROSTITUTE, approaches him silently. She pulls his cloak, smiling lasciviously.

MARIA TERESA (*V. O. cont.*): And they will be deported, the wretched women who live by selling themselves!

CASANOVA is attracted by the PROSTITUTE, but suddenly she runs away like a hare and disappears. From behind the corner of a house a MAN appears and stops to spy. He has a long sabre. ANOTHER MAN, also armed, pops out from the other side. They stand there motionless, watching. CASANOVA is worried. Over there, very far away the small figure of the PROSTITUTE crosses a road running, pursued by YET ANOTHER MAN with a drawn sabre.

CASANOVA (*V. O.*): The police of Vienna paid five hundred spies to disguise themselves in civilian clothing; and when a couple entered a house, the spy was keeping an eye on them.

CASANOVA glimpses a window, where in a dim light he sees a small feminine figure leaning out. A SPY comes towards CASANOVA in a determined way. CASANOVA, suddenly afraid, runs into the building of that lighted window.

INT. FLAT IN VIENNA. CORRIDOR. NIGHT.

CASANOVA (*V. O.*): I entered, running, into the flat while outside the shout of the police was growing faint. Here, in great astonishment . . .

A GIRL of about ten with very long, blonde hair, almost white, gives CASANOVA a small bow, then puts her index finger to her nose and beckons him to follow her.

INT. FLAT IN VIENNA. BEDROOM. NIGHT.

CASANOVA enters the bedroom lit by many candles. On the bed, there is an OLD MAN, dead. He is a sturdy, military type and has an ironic sneer still stamped on his lips.

The GIRL, every now and then speaks a sentence in German and takes an Austrian helmet and puts it down on the dead man's breast; then she takes a rifle, a sword, and a gun and puts everything beside the corpse as a tribute. CASANOVA looks around. There is a painting depicting a fierce officer (is he the dead man?), other portraits of the family, a Madonna, sensual and elegant, in Cranach's style.

The GIRL smiles at CASANOVA with melancholy and utters another brief sentence in German. Then she kneels down near the bed and recites the Paternoster. CASANOVA, puzzled, also kneels down and recites the prayer with the GIRL. Then he gets up.

INT. FLAT IN VIENNA. DINING ROOM. NIGHT.

CASANOVA enters the room. Everything is in order and very clean, motionless and quiet; no one is there.

INT. FLAT IN VIENNA. BEDROOM. NIGHT.

CASANOVA goes back to the GIRL. She is kissing the DEAD MAN'S forehead. She looks at him with a sweet smile, and sighs as if to say "Eh! How strange the life is!"

CASANOVA's eyes brim over with tears. He takes the GIRL in his arms and lifts her to his height.

CASANOVA: But you . . . are you all alone in this world? Is there anyone with you?

The GIRL doesn't understand, she answers with a laugh and another sentence in German. CASANOVA speaks more to himself than to the girl:

CASANOVA: You will be my daughter, then! (*impetuously*) You will come with me! You will always be with me! Do you want to come with me?

The GIRL seems to understand now: she goes and gets her cape. Then she takes the Madonna off the wall, puts it under her arm and holds her small hand out to CASANOVA, ready to go.

The DEAD MAN remains behind, with his ironic and malicious sneer.

INT./EXT. MOVING CARRIAGE. DAY.

The carriage is as wide as a small lounge, with a sofa on which CASANOVA and the GIRL are seated. Stirred by the movement of the carriage, baskets and bundles sway on the floor. The two are eating food that they have taken out of a small basket. They smile at each other. The GIRL points at something out the window and speaks in German, in her soft Austrian accent. Then she sighs, with a faint smile. CASANOVA nods in approval.

CASANOVA: I'll disclose to you the great secrets of nature. Together, we will travel our earthly way, I, trying to discover the great truths, and you, the small ones which are sometimes more beautiful. I will introduce you to the French king, and I'll read Dante to you. Of course you will study Italian. You, my little Viennese, don't look anything like me, but you seem to be my daughter anyway; though I haven't generated you, I have stolen you. Therefore you belong to me even more. Look!

CASANOVA suddenly falls silent and beats his stick to make the coachman stop. The carriage stops, CASANOVA jumps out, runs to a bush, picks a flower, runs back to the carriage, and hands it to the GIRL.

CASANOVA: An Eliocanthus!

INT. INN IN AUSTRIA OR SWITZERLAND IN THE MOUNTAINS. DINING ROOM. DAY.

The room has a big fireplace, hunting trophies, mugs, and barrels. The INNKEEPER, a blonde woman, is serving CASANOVA and the GIRL. They are seated at a long table. At another long table, there are TEN MEN, all young and handsome with blonde beards, who are eating cheerfully. Beside them are their rucksacks, rifles, and gun powder.

CASANOVA (*to the innkeeper*): Who are those men? Hunters?

The INNKEEPER shakes her head, laughing; then still laughing, but pretending to be scared.

INNKEEPER (*whispers*): Brigands!

She goes off, still laughing. CASANOVA amazed, looks at those elegant and happy MEN, who are now singing all together, marking time with their mugs.

INT. INN. CASANOVA'S ROOM. NIGHT.

The fire in the fireplace flares up. CASANOVA has scattered on the floor many women's dresses, shoes, and wigs. He claps his hands.

CASANOVA: Take off that miserable little dress! Here, for now you'll wear one of these larger dresses—they're a present I'm taking to a friend of mine in France—but then I'll buy you some clothes right for your age! Choose, now! This blue one? Or this silver dress?

The GIRL, half-naked, turns somersaults in the room, and on the bed, showing enthusiasm. Solemnly she puts on a grown woman's dress, even a pair of high-heeled shoes. She looks at herself in the mirror. Suddenly she is becoming serious, with a very elegant and detached air. She holds out her hand to CASANOVA. He kisses it with a perfect bow. He would like to caress her long silver hair, but he withdraws his hand shyly. The GIRL, scampering on the high heels, goes to hang her painting of The Madonna on the wall. She makes the sign of the cross.

CASANOVA (V. O.): I realized suddenly that she was exactly the woman who I perhaps could love.

From downstairs the music of a German chorus is coming. The brigands are singing. It is a sad piece, with some heartrending high notes.

The GIRL seems to know the music; at first she follows it, moving her hand, then singing in a weak, ill voice. CASANOVA pokes the fire in the fireplace and every now and then glances at the GIRL.

CASANOVA (V. O.): A fire in the fireplace has always made me want to be a small child and to walk unharmed into a cavern of embers, to climb on the live coal as in a phantasmagoria . . .

CASANOVA sits on an armchair near the fireplace and looks at the flame with deep sadness. Some times he turns and glances at the dresses scattered here and there.

The GIRL *has noticed Casanova's melancholy. She runs towards him with open arms. He opens his arms, she throws herself on him and covers his face with kisses.* CASANOVA *hugs her and returns the kisses that little by little are becoming more and more sensual: they are kisses of love.*

EXT. INN. DAY.

Casanova's carriage is in front of the inn's door. The INNKEEPER *and a* SERVANT *are loading the luggage.* CASANOVA *comes out of the house: he is by himself and frowning. He looks around, hesitating and decides to ask the* INNKEEPER, *with feigned ease:*

CASANOVA: That girl ... The girl who was with me ...

The INNKEEPER *looks at him smiling and says nothing.*

CASANOVA (*cont.*): Where is she? Have you seen her?

The INNKEEPER *laughs, shaking her head.*

INNKEEPER (suddenly): The brigands might have taken her with them!

She laughs loudly. CASANOVA *smiles faintly and gets in the carriage.*

CASANOVA (*to the coachman*): Go! And don't stop unless I tell you.

INT. LORD TALLOW'S PALACE IN ROME. HALL. NIGHT.

A spacious hall in a typical Baroque style palace, with a very high ceiling, frescoes, and paintings. In a corner there is a kneeling-stool. In the huge fireplace the fire blazes, but it seems that the room, too large, is rather cold.

LORD TALLOW, a tall Englishman with a cruel face, greets CASANOVA:

TALLOW: Welcome to Rome, dear Giacomo ... And thank you for accepting my invitation ... Tonight, though, we won't play ... Or rather, we won't play cards ...
CASANOVA: It doesn't matter, Milord. Your company is always pleasing. Is this palace yours?

TALLOW: The prince Orsini has rented it to me for one hundred pounds . . . his hams are included!

He points at a long table already set for dinner; along with many bottles of wine there are two whole hams, goats, and sausages.

A confused crowd of GUESTS is bustling around. In a corner, a small group of EUNUCHS, fat and tender like pigs, are singing in high voices creating a bizarre polyphony. There are beautiful and elegant LADIES speaking with a group of YOUNG WOMEN who are obviously prostitutes. CASANOVA is wandering around greeting PEOPLE and bowing, like a wolf looking for its prey; but he is anxious; he thought he would arouse more interest. Instead, everyone is minding his own business. Some GUESTS sit down at the table and start eating; others are eating near the fireplace, standing up. There is a disconnected foolish atmosphere. At a table in a corner some sturdy PEASANTS with crude, red faces are drinking quietly. A HALF-NAKED GIRL is dragging a YOUNG ABBOT by his hand. They move apart and the ABBOT starts to get undressed; he kisses his cross as he slips it off. Lord TALLOW caresses the face of ANOTHER ABBOT lasciviously, then kisses him.

The atmosphere is getting hotter. A handsome YOUNG MAN (perhaps also an abbot), who is holding a WOMAN in his arms, suggests:

YOUNG MAN (*loudly*): Let's have a contest! Let's bet who will be able to recognize me. To say between me and her, who is who? (*to the woman*) Quick, get undressed!

The YOUNG MAN and WOMAN get undressed in an alcove and lie face downwards on a couch, keeping their heads covered with cushions. A EUNUCH, laughing, opens the curtains uncovering two very similar bodies. Applause. The GUESTS crowd around, look, comment.

VOICES: That is a male ass . . . No, the other one . . . I bet one hundred sequins! Two hundred! That's the woman . . . The other one is smoother . . .

Everyone examines closely the buttocks of the two.

An OLD WOMAN, with a cruel air, goes close and starts feeling the two bottoms. Then suddenly she pinches one. The body wriggles. She pinches the other one even harder. Everybody laughs, but the two victims neither cry nor moan. She keeps pinching fiercely.

OLD WOMAN: I want them to scream . . . they have to scream . . .

CASANOVA, a man of the world, intervenes.

CASANOVA: You are breaking the rules, princess. This is not fair. And besides, there is no doubt. That one is the woman.

And CASANOVA, sure, turns over one of the bodies: it's a WOMAN. Applause, congratulations, laughs, screams. Some young MEN and WOMEN, encouraged by the example, frantically start to bare their buttocks in a frenzy of exhibitionism.

VOICES: Look at mine! This is really a female ass! . . . Mine is pink as the moon! . . . Here is a great ass, my friends! . . . Look but don't touch!

CASANOVA looks around, vacant, disgusted, offended. The guests haven't paid him any attention. He hasn't played cards. He is not enjoying himself. Perhaps it's better for him to leave. With nauseated pleasure, he kicks aside the things scattered on the floor: a broken bottle, pastry, a small stained shoe, underwear—all splashed with bodily fluids and wine . . .

CASANOVA heads for the exit. Before going out, he notices clothes piled up, a heap of wigs . . . He looks and leaves.

EXT. THE POPE'S PALACE OF THE QUIRINALE. GARDENS. DAY.

It is a beautiful, blue spring day in the gardens of the Quirinale. In a small lake a few majestic SWANS are swimming showing their long sensual necks. There are baroque and Greek statues of goddesses and well-developed young men. Some DOVES flutter about, cooing.

INT. GROTTO. DAY.

THE POPE is seated on a sedan chair, carried by TWO BEARERS in black, inside a shady, humid, and dripping grotto. He is fat and pinkish, and looks like a big, motherly, tired woman. Everything about him seems weary: he keeps his eyes almost closed, his hands resting on his stomach.

Around him MONSIGNORS and PRIESTS are walking, reading the breviary. A MONSIGNOR, with a deep bow to the POPE, announces:

MONSIGNOR: Giacomo Casanova.

CASANOVA kneels down, kisses the Pope's slipper. Then he rises keeping his humble, deferential, almost ecstatic attitude.

POPE (*in a honeyed, thin, female voice*): Ah, Giacomo . . . Eh, I have heard about you . . . Those poor inquisitors in Venice . . . What did you do to them?
CASANOVA: Your Holiness . . . I escaped, that's true . . . But I also repented . . . Besides . . . it's normal in men to try to avoid prison . . .
POPE (*gently*): But, what should I do now? Should I have you hanged? Eh?
CASANOVA (*worried*): Your Holiness . . . I hope that . . . My repentance . . . my humiliation . . . are . . .
POPE: But what are you doing these days? Have you married? Have you found a good girl?
CASANOVA: I don't think I have a bent for marriage. Even Saint Paul is in favor of celibacy . . .
POPE: Yes, but Saint Paul means a chaste celibacy, not one full of impure deeds like yours . . . I have learned that you are a great philanderer . . . Eh?

CASANOVA opens his arms.

CASANOVA: I recognize that I am a sinner. But who said, "Sin greatly, but love greatly"?
POPE: Martin Luther said that. You made a mistake and quoted a heretic . . .
CASANOVA: Then I'll quote Our Lord Jesus himself: "She will be forgiven because she has loved so much . . . "

The POPE shakes his head.

POPE: You young men, these days, you all are filled with modern, heretical, schismatic ideas . . . You think that the Gospel and St. Paul belong to you, that you may interpret them as you like . . . The Bible is ours. We alone can use it properly. If we give it to you, you will hurt yourself, like children with a razor ... Do you understand, my dear son?

CASANOVA's eyes brim over with tears.

CASANOVA: It is true! It is very true! Man is not able to steer himself ... or control himself ... He needs help ... a father and a mother ... restraint ... control ... Just yesterday, here, in this holy city of Rome ... If Your Holiness but knew!

CASANOVA sighs, moralistically.

POPE: What should I know?

CASANOVA takes on the air of a spy.

CASANOVA: A sinful meeting in the house of an English Lord ... I can mention his name ... my heart bled seeing so many horrible deeds committed, near your Holy See ... I ran away disgusted ... There were nobles, abbots, princes, princesses ...
POPE (*annoyed*): What nobles? What princesses? You must have been mistaken!

CASANOVA immediately understands his gaffe.

CASANOVA: Perhaps! Indeed, certainly! But I had very good intentions!
POPE: Don't look for the mote in you neighbor's eye. Look at the beam in your own!
CASANOVA: What a great truth, Holy Father ... Your words sink into my heart ... How I would like to confess, here in this celestial place ... in front of you, the Vicar of Our Lord ...
POPE: Please, confess, if you like.
CASANOVA (*bewildered*): How? Really? In front of Your Holiness?
POPE: Am I not a priest too?

MONSIGNORS and PRIESTS laugh politely, all the more so as the POPE has glanced around to make it clear that he has delivered a witticism.

CASANOVA: Holiness ... my mind is deranged ... My thousands of sins strike me in a tumult ... almost stifling me ... I ... have fornicated

... have killed even ... I have stolen ... All the divine laws of Moses and of Our Lord ... I have violated them all.

CASANOVA is sobbing, keeping his head down.

CASANOVA: I am filled with modern, sinful, and libertine ideas ... I believed in the freedom of men ... But now I know that the sweetest freedom is to open your soul to the Church ... to annihilate one's self in the divine body of the Church ...

CASANOVA raises his eyes and realizes that the Pope has left. He sees the sedan chair going away with the POPE. Amazed, he gets up. A PRIEST approaches him, putting his finger to his mouth.

PRIEST: He went to sleep. He always goes to sleep at this time.

EXT. VOLTAIRE'S VILLA IN SWITZERLAND. GARDEN. DAY.

A long, narrow table in the garden of Voltaire's villa in Switzerland. The GUESTS have just finished their lunch and are about to rise, when CASANOVA shows up. He goes to bow before VOLTAIRE, who is seated at the head of the table: old, with a malicious smile and a small cap like a skullcap on his head.

CASANOVA: This is the happiest moment of my life. Finally I am meeting my master. For twenty years I have been your devoted follower.
VOLTAIRE: Keep honoring me for another twenty, and promise to come to see me then ...

Everyone laughs loudly, excessively. CASANOVA is a little embarrassed.

CASANOVA: I promise, but you, for your part, must promise to wait for me.

Some laughter, but not as loud.

VOLTAIRE: I give you my word, and I would sooner die than not keep it.

More laughter; someone applauds. A beautiful, tall, dignified woman, ISABELLA, smiles, showing faint pity towards CASANOVA.

VOLTAIRE (*pressing*): Who is your favorite Italian poet?

CASANOVA: Ariosto; and I hope you have changed your mind about him. The harsh reviews you wrote. . . .

VOLTAIRE: I was young, I knew your language badly; I love Ariosto deeply.

CASANOVA: I can breathe now, Monsieur Voltaire. Please, then, retract your book that rendered Ariosto ridiculous.

VOLTAIRE: All my books are already banned.

The GUESTS keep laughing. CASANOVA grows red, and looks around lost. Then he meets the glance of ISABELLA, who is smiling with a touch of pity.

VOLTAIRE: It seems to me that you, on the contrary, are not at all excommunicated. Rather, you are almost in holy orders.

CASANOVA: Why do you say this?

VOLTAIRE: You told my friends a minute ago that you met the Pope, in Rome . . .

CASANOVA (*proud*): I had this honor. The current Pope is a lofty mind . . .

VOLTAIRE: But do you believe in God?

CASANOVA (*embarrassed*): I . . . I would like to discuss that with you . . .

VOLTAIRE (*smiling*): Once I had a lodge built in my garden. And I heard a mole talking with a beetle. "Here is a beautiful building, the mole was saying, It must be a most important mole that built this masterpiece." "You mistake yourself, said the beetle, It was a beetle full of genius that built this lodge." Since then, my friend, I have decided not to speak about God any longer.

CASANOVA has no answer and looks around for support, but no one is looking at him except for the smiling ISABELLA.

EXT. VOLTAIRE'S VILLA IN SWITZERLAND. GARDEN. DAY.

VOLTAIRE sleeps in his chair, with his head bent, half towards shadow, and half towards the sun. Several CATS are walking on the table, eating the leftovers in front of him. Some GUESTS, still seated, are chattering in low voices, eating hard-frozen sorbets. Others are walking in the garden. CASANOVA, seated at a table far from VOLTAIRE, is speaking to the beautiful, severe ISABELLA. They are drinking a red liquor, the bottle of which is in front of them.

ISABELLA: The duke of Villars, when he was old, became a woman.

ISABELLA nods towards an OLD GAUNT MAN with heavily made up, wan face. When he laughs he shows frightening, black teeth,

ISABELLA: (*cont.*): He suffers from gangrene. Every day, his doctor puts some stakes in his sore, and the disease devours them.
CASANOVA: And who is that Lady?

CASANOVA points at a LADY whose face is disfigured by a chocolate colored stains.

ISABELLA: The actress Dupuche. She can't perform any longer, since she had an effusion of milk, which caused her those spots on her face.
CASANOVA: I can see, Mr. Voltaire likes to receive artists and actors in his house.
ISABELLA: He wants his plays to be shown continuously in his villa; every room becomes a theater.
CASANOVA: A peculiar idea that, however, I find very interesting.

A BIG WOMAN, a wet-nurse, a maid, and a lover, comes to take VOLTAIRE to bed for his afternoon nap. VOLTAIRE, still asleep, lets her drag him, laying his small gaunt head on her enormous breasts.

ISABELLA: She is Madame Chatelet, his lover.
CASANOVA: Is she taking him to his bed or to his grave?
ISABELLA: To both places, I believe. But isn't she the kind of woman you also are looking for?
CASANOVA: Why do you say so?

ISABELLA smiles maliciously, mysteriously.

ISABELLA: I thought I had understood your taste. After what you have just told us, and thinking of what I was told about you, it seems that you live your loves like adolescent dreams.

ISABELLA gets up, and Casanova follows her.

EXT. VOLTAIRE'S VILLA IN SWITZERLAND. GARDEN. NIGHT.

MEN and WOMEN, some in contemporary clothes, others in ancient costumes are rehearsing Voltaire's tragedies: Brutus, Mohammed, *and some others.*

They recite the verses rhetorically, in very loud voices; but their faces express sincerity: some weep and sob, some laugh at the top of their voices, some menace, some sneer, others fall on their knees, others draw their swords; the women tear their hair. There is a violent, crazy atmosphere of uncontrolled feelings. CASANOVA and ISABELLA are among these mad people.

CASANOVA: I love women for what they are, my charming Isabella; and so I could love you too.

ISABELLA: I don't believe you. You don't understand women, as you do not understand yourself. Why do you run so quickly from one place to the next? Why?

CASANOVA: But . . . my business leads me. And also my loves which I pursue; I can't deny it. The attraction to women makes me rave.

ISABELLA: You don't pursue women. You run away from them. If you have loved so many women, perhaps it means that it is a man you are looking for . . .

CASANOVA (*laughing*): Oh! That's a good one! Your exquisite sex is the only one I am interested in.

ISABELLA: Why don't you marry?

CASANOVA: I fear marriage more than death.

ISABELLA: Then you don't love a woman, but women: that is, phantoms of women, that you, with your fickleness, wipe out in an instant.

CASANOVA: I feel that there is some truth to what you say; but you at least, sweet Isabella, don't be a phantom, and make me the happiest of men.

CASANOVA clasps Isabella's hand, looking in her eyes with great passion. Around them, the ACTORS and the ACTRESSES are miming similar scenes of false oaths and fake love affairs.

ISABELLA laughs and suddenly kisses CASANOVA on his mouth, withdrawing right after.

ISABELLA: Good, if you want to see me again, you will wait for me at the Mori hotel in Dresden.
CASANOVA (*passionately*): You are the only one I could really love . . . Oh, yes; for you I shall be able to give up this useless, boring freedom . . . I throw myself at your feet. Look: I kneel before your beauty, your intelligence, your . . .

CASANOVA falls to his knees, bowing his head to the ground, but when he lifts it up he realizes that Isabella has disappeared. Around him, the ACTORS keep playing their crazy scenes.

EXT./INT. MORI HOTEL IN DRESDEN. HALL. DAY.

There are many people in the hall: STRANGERS, SERVANTS, STABLE MEN; also some shady characters: THIEVES and PROSTITUTES.

CASANOVA (*V. O.*): I arrived at the Mori hotel in Dresden in a state of great agitation, since I was sure I had found the woman of my life, the one I was ready to marry . . . Isabella was twenty one, with a very white complexion and big black eyes like a nocturnal sky. Her great intelligence moreover, makes me consider her not only as a mate, but also as a friend with whom . . .

CASANOVA has entered the hotel and is asking about ISABELLA. But the INNKEEPER is shaking his head: the woman hasn't arrived yet. CASANOVA looks around lost, not knowing what to do.

CASANOVA (*V. O.*): That woman had won me over; in her arms I felt like an inexperienced child, who consents to be led toward . . .
FEMALE VOICE (*O. S.*): Giacomo!

We see a mature woman, ASTRODI, approaching CASANOVA. She is accompanied by a female hunchback, SUSANNA, with very long legs.

CASANOVA: We have met before, I believe . . .
ASTRODI: I am the actress Astrodi that you abandoned. And this is Susanna, a friend of mine; she is also an actress and a very lively ballerina.

CASANOVA looks at the hunchback's face with a sort of foul attraction; it is full of life, joy, and sensuality.

ASTRODI: We are here for tomorrow's show of *Orpheus and Eurydice*. But wouldn't you like to have dinner with us tonight?

ASTRODI smiles clearly with whorish intent. Even the hunchback SUSANNA is smiling.

CASANOVA stiffens in resistance.

CASANOVA (*shouts*): No! Not this! I have an appointment here! I . . .

But immediately SUSANNA comes closer to CASANOVA, sticks her tongue out and pokes it in his mouth in a long and vampire like kiss.

CASANOVA (*V. O.*): . . . Astrodi placed a pillow in such a way that we could carry the act out easily . . . even though the hunchback had her head pressed to her breast . . .

INT. MORI HOTEL IN DRESDEN. CASANOVA'S ROOM. DAY.

CASANOVA, ASTRODI, and SUSANNA, all together in bed, commit complicated, odd, and monstrous sexual acts.

INT. THEATER IN DRESDEN. NIGHT.

ASTRODI, the hunchback SUSANNA and the ENTIRE TROUPE are presenting the ballet Orpheus and Eurydice. *The backdrop is a forest full of horses, goats, tigers, chickens, elephants, snakes, donkeys, and giraffes. All these painted animals stare at the audience.*

At the end of the dance, ORPHEUS, with his lyre, EURYDICE and the GODS bow with a great flourish. The public is applauding them.

Then everyone suddenly turns and bows together toward the royal box. It seems that the PRINCE OF SAXONY doesn't notice this. He is leaving with his COURTIERS.

CASANOVA, in the orchestra, also bows toward the prince, with a conventional smile.

The theater is emptying out; the last people are leaving from the small side doors.

CASANOVA is almost by himself in the empty theater, the curtain is still open, and from the backdrop the painted animals keep staring at the orchestra.

The lights are turned off. In the silence, a female voice resounds, a little harsh and old.

OLD WOMAN: Giacomo!

CASANOVA, confused, looks up: an OLD WOMAN seated in a box seat, her appearance and clothes are almost regal; she could be a queen mother.

OLD WOMAN (*in a mixture of Venetian and German accents*): Giacomo! Don't you recognize me? I recognized you at once, stupid!

CASANOVA gives a startled and even slightly scared smile.

CASANOVA: Mother! Is it you?
OLD WOMAN: It's me. Didn't you know that I live in Dresden? I have a pension of four hundred thalers, God save the prince! (*She says this last sentence in German*).
CASANOVA: I knew that you were in Saxony. I'm here on business. I have a project which interests the minister greatly.
OLD WOMAN: I understand ... The usual nonsense. The usual cheating. Der Teufel! And never a penny for your mother, poor old woman.

CASANOVA, coming closer to the box, is now humble and almost loving.

CASANOVA: I would have liked to write you; to go see you. But I didn't know your address. How is your second husband?
OLD WOMAN: Dead.

The OLD WOMAN makes the sign of the cross.

CASANOVA: Do you live in Dresden?
OLD WOMAN: I live in the country.
CASANOVA: I could come to see you. I could stay with you for a few

days. If my business allows me.
OLD WOMAN: Come to my place? Stay with me?

She laughs—a sinister and wicked laugh. CASANOVA is muddled. He goes even to the box.

CASANOVA: What are you doing up there?
OLD WOMAN: I'm waiting for them to come and pick me up. I am an invalid and can't walk.
CASANOVA: Wait, I'll come up, I'll take you home myself.

CASANOVA goes up quickly through a small side staircase, and enters the box. He takes up his mother in his arms. She looks suddenly very small: a small heap of rags.

CASANOVA sets off with the OLD WOMAN through the corridors of the theater; in the meantime, with her small wrinkled hand she caresses her son's face, muttering incomprehensible, ironically affectionate words.

EXT. THEATER IN DRESDEN. NIGHT.

Outside the theater door, lit by reddish wandering torches and lamps, stands CASANOVA. He carries the OLD WOMAN—his mother in his arms like a parcel. He speaks to her, but looks straight ahead, absorbed.

CASANOVA: You are mistaken in saying that I am just a buffoon. My name is well known all over Europe; I am considered a scholar and a shrewd businessman of great genius. I possess four hundred gold coins of which I am willing to give you half. But I'm not that young any longer, and I intend to stop running around the world. I'd like to find a house in the countryside, perhaps near yours. It could be an attractive possibility for me. First, though, I must make a very important negotiation. When I come to see you I will tell you everything. Have you heard lately from our relatives in Venice? I hope to go back to Venice as soon as the inquisitors . . .

A carriage arrives unexpectedly, and stops in front of them. A young German SERVANT gets out quickly and hastens to take the OLD WOMAN from Casanova's arms.

She is taken to the carriage, the COACHMAN whips the HORSES, and the carriage sets off at a gallop.

CASANOVA, taken aback by such a rapid abduction.

CASANOVA (*shouts*): Mother!

Then he smiles and shrugs his shoulders muttering:

CASANOVA: She didn't even give me her address . . .

He slowly sets out on foot. A little later we hear his voice singing a lively romance, almost a war song. Then he stops singing and slowly moves into the darkness:

CASANOVA (*V. O.*): My mother . . . I never saw her again . . . And she never knew that, thanks to me, she was already a grandmother. To be honest, I didn't know then either that I had a daughter . . .

INT. ROYAL PALACE IN NAPLES. HALL. DAY.

A hall in the royal palace of the king of Naples, Ferdinand I, crowded with COURTIERS and LADIES. The young, nineteen-year-old KING, half naked, is jumping on a big blanket held by four sturdy MEN, who, as he lands, pull it tight, tossing the KING two or three meters high. The CROWD OF COURTIERS screams rhythmically:

CROWD: Long live the king!

The KING, out of breath, sweaty, and happy, jumps to the ground.

KING (*shouting*): Now it's the queen's turn! Come on!

The QUEEN, also very young, covers her face with a fan and runs away laughing. Some OLD COURTIERS, scared of being chosen, go away limping.

The KING, still laughing, points at a young BLONDE GENTLEMAN.

KING: English ambassador! Do you want to play?

The BLONDE GENTLEMAN takes a small bow, then, sportingly, undresses and jumps on the blanket. The MEN pull the blanket tight, and the ambassador is catapulted into the air, amid the laughs and screams of the COURTIERS. CASANOVA is among them; he laughs and approves of the childish game.

CASANOVA: The court of Naples is, without doubt, the most cheerful of Europe. A young king brings joy of life, happiness and liveliness to the entire realm. Long life to King Ferdinand!

He applauds. Meanwhile the BLONDE GENTLEMAN—the English ambassador—is falling awkwardly out of the blanket; but he immediately gets up, with an elegant jump.

The KING points at TWO OLD MEN, hunchbacked in front as well as behind.

KING: You come from Florence, if I'm not wrong . . .
HUNCHBACKS (*together*): To honor your Majesty.
KING: Good. Now you will honor me by playing ball: you are going to be the balls!

All the COURTIERS laugh loudly. The TWO OLD MEN, the hunchbacks, resigned, anxious, get undressed and manage to jump into the blanket. They are tossed in the air. The scene is macabre and absurd.

CASANOVA is laughing ostentatiously, servile. A small, pot-bellied man approaches him with a pale face and and sarcastic expression. He is the DUKE OF MATALONA.

MATALONA: Since you seem to like this stupid game so very much, why don't you ask to be tossed in the air?

CASANOVA: I would do it, if the king asked me.
MATALONA: So do you do only what you are asked?

CASANOVA flares up.

CASANOVA: Sir, I don't know you well enough to permit such a joke.

MATALONA becomes hypocritically humble: it is clear that he's trying to make fun of CASANOVA.

MATALONA: But what are you saying? I sincerely admire you. If I were a woman I would have already made love to you. I've heard great things . . .

Playing the fool, MATALONA touches Casanova's fly. CASANOVA smiles pleased.

CASANOVA: I am proud of the admiration of a gentleman like you.
MATALONA: They speak of you as being like of a horse, or some other noble animal.
CASANOVA (*offended*): What do you mean?
MATALONA: But from this point of view, of course!

And MATALONA again touches Casanova's fly, amid everyone's laughter. CASANOVA, indignant, is about to leave.

CASANOVA: Your crude jokes don't amuse me. Duke Matalona, my respects.

DUKE MATALONA follows him, suddenly anxious; he seizes him by the arm, caressing his hand like a child who wants to be forgiven.

MATALONA: Wait . . . Don't leave angry . . . Can I have the honor of inviting you to my house?

INT. MATALONA'S CARRIAGE. NIGHT.

Pressed one against the other on the seat of the duke's carriage, CASANOVA and MATALONA talk. MATALONA displays an odd agitation, like a nagging worry that he is trying vainly to conceal.

MATALONA: Five years ago . . . no, ten or even more . . . Forgive my confusion, dear Casanova! You have been to Naples, haven't you?
CASANOVA: Certainly. And if I am not wrong, I've already had the pleasure of meeting you.
MATALONA: The pleasure! No, mine! Only mine! Then . . . then, though, we didn't see each other very often. I was always by myself, in despair . . . I suffered the pains of love! You know the pains of love!

CASANOVA nods, as an expert.

CASANOVA: There are sufferings that also give much delight, the delight of being alive, of loving, even though the love unluckily is not reciprocated ...

MATALONA: And so it was my case! The woman that I loved passionately was married. But her husband wasn't an obstacle, no; the trouble was that she fell in love with another, who seduced and abandoned her ... and I suffered doubly ... for my unhappiness and for that of my sweetheart Lucrezia ...

CASANOVA frowns, pensive.

CASANOVA: Lucrezia?

MATALONA grows red with anger and suddenly attacks shrilly:

MATALONA: You were that seducer, Casanova!

CASANOVA (*raises his voice*): I will not tolerate being addressed in this tone!

MATALONA quickly reverts to his hypocritical humility:

MATALONA: I beg your pardon, dear friend. Forgive a poor irascible old man ...

He rubs his face and begins speaking again in a quiet tone:

MATALONA: A little later her husband died ... My poor Lucrezia agreed to marry me, even though she's never loved me ... But now she's my wife. I am taking you to her!

MATALONA laughs nervously.

CASANOVA: Duke, frankly I don't understand you. You know our past. I can see you're still jealous. You want to take me to Lucrezia? Why?

MATALONA (*in a low voice, almost whispering*): Because you are the only one who can get your memory out of her heart ... because all these years she's been in love with you ... and I want you to speak to her ... And moreover I want her to see you again ... as you are today. Old! And ugly!

MATALONA stares at CASANOVA with an odd intensity, so that CASANOVA is stunned and speechless.

INT. DUKE MATALONA'S VILLA. HALL. NIGHT.

In the hall of the villa, LUCREZIA, a beautiful woman of thirty-eight, is playing the spinet, accompanying CASANOVA who stands beside her, singing a romance. He does it in an inspired manner, but his voice, not young any more, is hoarse and tired.

MATALONA is still seated at the table, where we see the leftovers of their dinner; he is drunk, his head propped on his hand, a glass of wine is in front of him. LUCREZIA goes on playing; every now and then she glances at CASANOVA and smiles.

As CASANOVA finishes singing, his voice breaks on a trill. LUCREZIA turns towards her husband.

LUCREZIA: You should be ashamed of yourself! Even tonight you get drunk.
MATALONA (*whinnying like a guilty child*): Forgive me, my Lucrezia . . . Only a glass or two in honor of our guest . . .

LUCREZIA speaks to him with spite and hatred.

LUCREZIA: You know it disgusts me to see you this way. Go. Go away!

The DUKE MATALONA gets up staggering; immediately a SERVANT arrives to steady him and takes him away.

LUCREZIA and CASANOVA are seated side by side on a sofa.

LUCREZIA (*smiling sweetly*): Your image has comforted me during all these years of unhappiness with a man I hate.
CASANOVA: But why did you marry him?
LUCREZIA (*sighing*): Alone, with a daughter, in dire financial straits, I didn't have any choice.
CASANOVA: Is your daughter beautiful?
LUCREZIA: You mean our daughter.

CASANOVA jumps to his feet.

CASANOVA: For heaven sake, what are you saying?
LUCREZIA: It's the truth, Leonilda is your daughter; I'm sure. Even my first husband knew that and called her Giacomina as a joke. The Duke Matalona, on the other hand, knows nothing.
CASANOVA: But couldn't she be the duke's daughter? I know that he also courted you at that time.
LUCREZIA (*with scorn*): He never had me. Neither then nor after.
CASANOVA: What! Not even after you married?
LUCREZIA: The duke is completely impotent ... For that very reason he hates you ... Wait ... I hear a carriage ... It is Leonilda. She's coming back from the royal ball.

A girl of sixteen, LEONILDA, with a melancholy face, all wrapped up, enters. She bows to CASANOVA without smiling. LUCREZIA with a broad gesture points at him.

LUCREZIA: Leonilda, this is your father! Give him a hug.

LEONILDA, without showing anxiety and still without smiling, goes to kiss CASANOVA on his check. He holds her tight, touched and happy.

INT. DUKE MATALONA'S VILLA. BEDROOM. NIGHT.

The room where Casanova is hosted has a tall huge bed, like a scow. LUCREZIA and CASANOVA, a little drunk, very cheerful, are pushing each other affectionately; he is caressing her.

CASANOVA: You are still firm, and beautiful ... get undressed like that time in Tivoli ...

She pushes him away laughing; then she puts her finger in his hair.

LUCREZIA: I'll be your maid. I'll loosen your hair.
CASANOVA: Then you also have to undress me.

CASANOVA sniggers, a bit inebriated and dazed, while LUCREZIA undresses him, laying bare his body now getting old, with white hairs on his chest. She gives him small and sensual kisses on his neck and on his chest.

LUCREZIA: This is a dream that is finally coming true. All these years I've been waiting for this moment . . .

CASANOVA (*a bit mournful*): But, don't you find me old? Don't I disgust you?

LUCREZIA: I love you more than ever.

The two kiss with passion.

CASANOVA: Now you have to get undressed too . . . I'll take care of it!

CASANOVA is about to undress LUCREZIA, when a voice stops him:

VOICE: No, I will.

In the dark room LEONILDA has appeared. She is no longer wrapped up, but wears a low-cut dress. She still has a melancholy and mysterious look, somewhat offended and wounded, but now a strong sensuality glares in her eyes.

LUCREZIA laughs.

LUCREZIA: Well! Do you want to undress me? And why not? It's amusing!

LEONILDA starts slowly to undress her mother, even lightly caressing her breasts and her hips. In the meantime CASANOVA wraps his hair in a kerchief and lies on the bed.

CASANOVA: Be quick about it! Here, on the bed, the whole family will get together!

LUCREZIA: Ah, no. You will take care only of me.

LEONILDA: But I'll be present. And you . . . as my father . . . you will have to see me too . . . And you'll become fully aware of your handiwork!

LEONILDA, too, gets undressed: she has a nice slender figure she is proud of. CASANOVA and LUCREZIA make love. LEONILDA watches them greedily, then hugs them both, in an affectionate, daughter-like gesture, and begins to moan with excitement.

LEONILDA (*in a broken voice*): Ah that's what it is . . . It is like that that you conceived me . . . Like that . . .

All the sudden she gets frantic, and starts pushing her mother away:

LEONILDA: Go! Go away . . . Go away . . . I . . . I'm here . . .

LUCREZIA, *pushed away, is stunned.*

LUCREZIA: No! What are you doing? Leonilda, not you! He is your father!

But LEONILDA is already clinging to CASANOVA, weeping sensuous tears. CASANOVA, not even trying to restrain himself, embraces and kisses his daughter; as he possesses her, she gives out a cry of pain.

INT. DUKE MATALONA'S VILLA. BEDROOM. DAWN.

CASANOVA sleeps alone on the big bed. Lucrezia and Leonilda have left. Only one faint light is still on. Casanova's sleep is restless; he seems oppressed by nightmares. Every now and then he moans. There's an atmosphere of suspense: something dramatic is going to happen. In fact, shadows are advancing cautiously: they are Matalona's SERVANTS, each carrying a stick. CASANOVA seems to have a premonition of the danger, because he suddenly wakes up to see the SERVANTS approaching him threateningly.

CASANOVA: What's going on? Who are you? What do you want?

All of a sudden, the SERVANTS hurl themselves at CASANOVA and start beating him savagely. CASANOVA, screaming, tries to defend himself. From the door, MATALONA, pale and sweaty in a dressing gown, looks on.

CASANOVA catches sight of him.

CASANOVA (*shouts*): Filthy traitor! Scoundrel! Damned impotent!
MATALONA (*sneering*): Impotent . . . you too . . . just wait . . .

INT. WÜRTTEMBERG CASTLE. DUKE OF WÜRTTEMBERG'S ROOM. DAY.

The room is very large. It serves as bedroom, bathroom and audience-hall. Casanova's voice is heard. It has come to sound more tired, hoarse, heavy.

CASANOVA (*V. O.*): The most brilliant court in Europe was, at that time, that of the duke of Wurttemberg.

There are a lot of people in the room: OFFICERS, SERVANTS, MAIDS. A BALLERINA is dancing, moving here and there: she is wearing the costume of a Greek goddess.

CASANOVA (*V. O.*): The duke never held himself back: hunting, dances, theater . . . He rarely slept, thought is was a waste of time, and his servants were instructed to do anything necessary to wake him up.

The DUKE, a short, stocky man with a hard, military face, is in bed and having difficulty waking up. A pretty and flirtatious MAID has her arm around his neck, trying to open his mouth and to make him gulp a big cup of coffee. The DUKE takes a gulp, then lunging, seizes the MAID and with an obscene kiss passes the coffee from his mouth to hers. She laughs, spewing the coffee all around. The DUKE falls back on the pillows.

The COURT DOCTOR, an old man with a white wig and a red face, approaches. He lifts the DUKE'S eyelid, bending to examine the eye.

DOCTOR: He is still drunk.

He beckons to two SERVANTS, who roughly seize the DUKE by his arms and drag him out of his bed.

DUKE: Scoundrels . . . put me down. I'll have you hanged.

Rudely the SERVANTS drop him in a tub full of cold water. The DUKE gives a scream, then bursts out laughing and starts splashing the water as he picks his way through a German military song.

Some CLOWNS enter the room. They look sinister. The FIRST CLOWN has two huge fake hunchbacks; one in front, one in the back. The SEC-

OND CLOWN has fake genitals made of red material: two big balls and a penis like a soft, stuffed roll, which, every now and then he uses to beat people, especially women. The THIRD CLOWN is dressed up like a peasant woman, with a large straw hat and two baskets. She is the tallest and has a moustache. The OTHER CLOWN keeps taking off and putting on the mask of a gorilla.

The CLOWNS invade the room screaming, yammering rapidly, singing and beating and pushing everyone else. The DUKE laughs, while a CHAMBERLAIN approaches him.

CHAMBERLAIN: Your Excellency, it's time for the hearings.

While the CLOWNS keep playing their gloomy tricks, an OLD OFFICER, almost shouting, accuses a PEASANT who stands alone confused.

OFFICER: Here he is, the man who sheared my sheep! Three bags of wool he stole, Excellency! He is a good-for-nothing, always drunk, beats his wife! I've had him beaten already, but it was all in vain. I ask you: make an example of him!

The DUKE, in the tub, dozes off. The CHAMBERLAIN walks to him and, respectfully but soundly, slaps him twice. The DUKE wakes up.

CHAMBERLAIN (*with respect*): Which punishment do you wish to inflict on the serf Martin Rausch?
DUKE (*screaming*): Hang him! Hang him!

CASANOVA enters the room, looks around surprised and curious, and bows low to the DUKE. Now he is a mature man, a bit paunchy. He continues to deport himself with dignity, but he is changing for the worse ...

CHAMBERLAIN: Mr. Giacomo Casanova, knight of Seingalt, from Venice.
DUKE: Hang him also!

CASANOVA makes a gesture of offended dignity.

CASANOVA: Please! I am here to see you, Excellency. I am bringing a letter from Cardinal Louvier. And a proposal for a big financial enterprise: a lottery of a new kind.

The CLOWN, the one with the fake genitals, goes close to CASANOVA and strikes him a blow with his stuffed penis. CASANOVA immediately reacts: he draws his sword, and strikes him with the flat of the blade. The CLOWN falls backwards. Everyone laughs. CASANOVA smiles, satisfied.

INT./EXT. WÜRTTEMBERG CASTLE. DINING ROOM. GARDEN. NIGHT.

The DUKE, his FRIENDS, COURTIERS, and OFFICERS are seated at the table with faces red from the wine and the beer. Some OFFICERS behave vulgarly, and crudely groping the LADIES, who laugh.

CASANOVA, by comparison, behaves like a gentleman: eats politely, smiles, and speaks with animation. He feels disorientated by the rude atmosphere. We get a glimpse of a LADY, also seated at the table, who has a small black mask on her eyes and sits very properly, motionless. A SERVANT enters the room holding directly in his gloved hands an enormous roasted duck: he puts it in the middle of the table, within a platter full of red sauce.

ONE OF THE CLOWNS is chasing a MAID who enters carrying a tray full of food; he puts his hand under her dress, she screams, and drops the tray. The CLOWN grabs her by her waist, they fall and roll about on the floor, and everyone laughs.

Suddenly, TWO OFFICERS at the table, for an unknown reason burst out shouting, insulting, and threatening each other in German. They stand up and leave with stiff, military strides.

They go into the garden near the dining room. They stand face to face, then draw their guns and immediately fire. One of them falls to the ground with his forehead split open. The other goes back to the dining room. The killing has happened with startling rapidity and with total indifference of the others present.

The DUKE is about to put a leg of pheasant in his mouth, but a CLOWN behind him, takes it from his hand. The DUKE seizes the clown's hand and holds it tight over a candle's flame. The CLOWN screams while everyone else goes on laughing.

In the confusion, CASANOVA speaks aloud to no one in particular; and in fact no one is listening.

CASANOVA: The Piombi prison in Venice, gentlemen, isn't, of course, like your prisons here in Germany, although I like to think that I would be able to escape even from one of your dreadful fortresses. What are you saying? Why escape? Oh, I know very well that there are people who don't like to escape, and when they are in prison they would never leave, not even if they were kicked out, because there they have the comfort of free food and lodging, and even a lot of wine, if they can pay for it. I instead . . . escaped. I escape continually, from one place to the next. This world is a prison, don't you agree? And not being able to escape completely, I move about in this enormous cell . . . What? What are you saying? No, my philosophy condemns suicide. I am a good Catholic, after all. Besides, suicide is for dullards: for people without imagination. What do you think, beautiful lady?

The LADY to whom he is speaking puts an oyster on the tip of her tongue and spitefully holds it out to CASANOVA, who, immediately attracted, takes the oyster with his lips and kisses the LADY passionately. The LADY who is wearing the little black mask is still motionless, but her head is slightly bent. It seems that the MOTIONLESS LADY smiles with a light irony at CASANOVA.

Suddenly the DUKE speaks to CASANOVA with a sarcastic smile and the expression of someone who is preparing a joke.

DUKE: Knight of Seingalt! You are a famous suitor of beautiful women. But you are behaving with no gallantry to the Countess Rosalba!

The DUKE points with a broad gesture at the MOTIONLESS LADY. She slowly turns her head toward Casanova, lifts her arm and slowly takes off the mask, showing a round, pale face. CASANOVA is confused: the strange, perhaps ill, woman, strikes him.

DUKE (*cont.*): All night long you haven't smiled at her. Do you want her to cry? She is so sensitive!

CASANOVA bends over the person next to him.

CASANOVA (*whispers*): Who is she? Is she ill?

Suddenly, from the MOTIONLESS LADY's eyes (we now see that she is a mechanical doll) big tears start to fall, many drops stain her face and fall on her breasts and on her dress; all around laughter bursts out. CASANOVA stands up and goes closer to the doll in admiration.

CASANOVA: Enchanting! I have heard of something like that in Nuremburg, where a rich general had a chess player built for him. But this one goes beyond all imagination!

CASANOVA bends over the doll looking at her closely.

CASANOVA (*cont.*): By Jove! One would think that she is made of flesh: her complexion could deceive anyone.

CASANOVA touches her neck. The doll lifts her arm and slaps him while all the GUESTS laugh.

DUKE: And this is not all! I also own, for my pleasure, a white monkey from the West Indies . . .

A cage set on four wheels arrives. Inside is a horrible MONKEY that fiercely bares its teeth, and is masturbating.

INT. WÜRTTEMBERG CASTLE. DINING ROOM. NIGHT.

The room is half-lit and deserted. Everything is still as it was at the end of the dinner; dirty dishes, half full glasses, chairs left around . . . The mechanical doll—MOTIONLESS LADY—is still there in her seat. CASANOVA, in a dressing gown and night cap, cautiously enters the room and approaches the doll as if bewitched. He laughs, a forced laugh that resounds icily in the room. He makes a deep bow.

CASANOVA: Good night, madam. Why still up?

He carefully examines her. Her face is pale, but painted broadly with red and black, like a clown. Her glass eyes gaze blankly into space. Yet, beyond her lack of expression, she ironically, seems to allude to something mysterious, unreachable: like the cold smile of the Mona Lisa.

CASANOVA *feels her breasts. After a little while the MOTIONLESS LADY slaps him. He jumps backward, puzzled. Then, hesitating, he goes closer again and, lifting her gently, puts her on her feet and walks around her, studying her. He presses some buttons. A music is coming from inside the doll; it sounds like a music box, a bit jumpy, but sweet. The doll gives a gentle bow, then starts to spin in a circle, dancing to the rhythm of the music. CASANOVA keeps walking around her, as if he were dancing with her. His dressing gown flutters around him, as does her magnificent dress around her mechanical body.*

INT. WÜRTTEMBERG CASTLE. CASANOVA'S BEDROOM. DINING ROOM. NIGHT.

The doll is lying in bed, in an unnatural and uncomfortable pose, sunk in the feather mattress. CASANOVA is all excitement, captivated by this new experience. He presses a button in her waist. The doll sits up a little and slowly opens her arms. Caressing her face, arms and feet, he recites with great emphasis Petrarch's verses:

CASANOVA: The eyes, the arms, the hands, the feet, the face,
Which made my thoughts and words so warm and wild,
That I was almost from myself exiled,
And render'd strange to all the human race;
The lucid locks that curl'd in golden grace,
The lightening beam that, when my angel smiled,
Diffuse o'er earth an Eden heavenly mild . . .

Suddenly the doll closes her arms, clasping CASANOVA, who kisses her on the lips, then draws back, upset. He slowly takes his dressing gown off, remaining half-naked. Then, very slowly, he undresses her.

CASANOVA: I beg your pardon, madam, for taking these liberties. I wanted to see how you appeared in the eyes of your creator. Don't say anything. What sort of a crazy inventor was your father? He must have been a poet as well, because he made you so beautiful. Could he have slept with you too, incestuous man? Don't answer, my love. Offer your mechanism to my sensual pleasure.

CASANOVA opens her legs.

CASANOVA (*whispering*): Tin legs . . .

His face flaming with lust, he tries to rape the doll. Her face makes mechanical movements: she opens and closes her eyes, turning her head to right and left. CASANOVA, sweating, scarcely manages to make love to the doll.

He remains still, as if he were dead. When he gets up his face is tense and deathly pale. Carefully, gently, as if he were recomposing a dead body, he puts the doll's limbs back and settles her properly on the bed, like a corpse.

He starts to get dressed.

CASANOVA: (*V. O.*): Immediately thereafter, I went to Spain, to Barcelona . . . The next year the English Secretary sent me to Livorno well recommended . . . to sail to Constantinople with the Russian fleet . . . I went to the Congress of Augusta on a mission from the King of Portugal . . .

EXT. MOVING CARRIAGE. BOHEMIA'S COUNTRY SIDE. DAY.

A small and gloomy carriage moves through a prairie covered with snow. From the small window CASANOVA's face leans out, melancholy.

CASANOVA (*V. O.*): Then I decided to go to Berlin, but halfway there Count Waldenstein stopped me and took me to Dux, where I have lived ever since, and where to all appearances I shall die . . .

INT. CASTLE AT DUX. KITCHEN. NIGHT.

The kitchen is spacious, with many fireplaces, spits, barrels, skinned animals, sharp knives, and shining carving-forks. MAIDS and COOKS with loose dresses, bonnets, and velvet bodices. Lighting makes the blades, copper pans, and crystal glasses shine. The wood of a very long table, also shines from many years of use. In short, a typical German–Flemish room, blazing and glittering, infernal and domestic. The SERVANTS, MAIDS and HOUSEKEEPER—a mixed world of different ages and sexes—are seated at the table, where tureens, roasts and bottles of wine are set. Among them, there is a camaraderie of jokes and chatter.

But CASANOVA, lonely, old and shaky, in a long shabby coat, comes and sits down at the side of the table. He has a sulky, scornful expression, but with a sort of resignation like a dog used to whipping.

While the SERVANTS cheerfully eat, CASANOVA sips his soup in silence. No one looks at him. Suddenly he starts pounding his hand on the table in a sort of drumming.

CASANOVA: My macaroni! I want my macaroni!

An old and motherly COOK rushes up to CASANOVA.

COOK: Tonight I didn't fix macaroni, sir; I prepared goat's offal.
CASANOVA (*with indignation*): I don't care. I've clearly told you that I want my macaroni every night. If that is not possible, the count will be informed. That's enough. Go away!

The COOK, feeling bad, tries to make amends.

COOK: There's polenta: it will be ready in a few minutes.

CASANOVA smiles bitterly.

CASANOVA: No, no ... The polenta isn't important ... Furthermore, I can't stand ...

CASANOVA looks toward the other side of the table, where an old steward FELTKIRCHNER, an old man with a coarse, cruel military look sits surrounded by his noisy OFFICERS, among whom are some EFFEMINATE MEN.

CASANOVA (*cont.*): ... my dinner being spoilt by those loud scums!

Only now does FELTKIRCHNER seem to notice Casanova's presence.

FELTKIRCHNER: Mr. Casanova! I thought we agreed you would leave after the roast. Why are you still here?

CASANOVA, furious, gets up and, trembling with rage, goes over to his enemy.

CASANOVA: Listen, Feltkirchner! Only one of life's many oddities has allowed us to meet like this: I librarian, you steward! Respect my solitude, stay away from me, you arrogant, scheming . . . You're taking advantage of the count's absence . . . But he will know!

FELTKIRCHNER says something in German to his FRIENDS, clearly something scornful about Casanova. They look at him and snigger. CASANOVA is beside himself with anger.

CASANOVA: You even indulge in unnatural, perverted passions! You and Videral! I loathe you both!

VIDERAL, a young man with a wicked, ugly face, jumps to his feet, shouting something in German at CASANOVA, who, by now tired and bored, ceases grumbling.

CASANOVA: Go on, speak your German slang . . . who can understand you? I'm an artist. I'm a writer and librarian. I don't mingle with people like you.

FELTKIRCHNER: Mr. Videral is not just a valet, he is also an artist: a talented actor!

CASANOVA: It's disgusting!

FELTKIRCHNER (*shouts to him*): Don't play haughty; you're a servant of Count Waldstein just like us!

CASANOVA leaves.

CASANOVA (*repeating*): Disgusting. Disgusting.

INT. CASTLE AT DUX. LAVATORY. DAY.

CASANOVA, like a museum guide, is showing a group of old GENTLE-MEN around. They are taciturn and look like village notables. He opens a small lavatory door.

CASANOVA (*solemnly*): Here the most dreadful insult to me took place. They tore my portrait from one of my books and stuck it here with filth.

They all look, showing interest and without laughing, at a sheet of paper with Casanova's portrait, stuck up on the lavatory's door and stained with excrement.

CASANOVA (*cont.*): The offender is Feltkirchner, or his friend Videral: we don't know to whom the fecal substance belongs . . . The awful relationship that exists between them . . . makes the mixture of that stuff easy . . .

The GENTLEMEN observe seriously, making brief remarks in a low voice. CASANOVA is almost proud of such a great offense.

CASANOVA: Look at it; take your time . . . it's a very lifelike portrait. It's printed on my famous novel *Icosameron*. Have you read it, by chance? I'll take the liberty of offering a copy of it to each of you. I believe that after my death, they'll speak of me as the author of this book for a long time . . .

While the GENTLEMEN march away silently. CASANOVA smiles, pleased though in the end mortified, beaten.

CASANOVA: I am a famous Italian writer . . . You know my name, surely . . . Giacomo Casanova, from Venice, scholar, philosopher . . . And that was my portrait . . .

INT. CASTLE AT DUX. COUNTESS'S BEDROOM. DAY.

The COUNTESS, mother of Waldstein is seated in an armchair near a window. Beyond the pane, divided in small rectangles, we catch sight of a stretch of snow, from which a few black bare trees pop out. Even the old COUNTESS is in some way skeleton-like and mournful; very pale, gaunt, she wears black and stares at the window wrapped in a sad meditation. She is a mournful image of the nearness of death (her death or Casanova's?)

CASANOVA enters and gives her a humble bow.

CASANOVA: It is not to indulge any whim that I come to you, but to beseech justice; justice for a poor, old man . . .

CASANOVA has tears in his eyes; the COUNTESS sighs.

CASANOVA: For six weeks my portrait has been stuck up on the lavatory door by repugnant matter ... The vile Feltkirchner and his thug Videral have been tormenting me on every excuse: they've even made a skeleton key with which they can enter the library and steal books, for whose disappearance they blame me ... I haven't had macaroni since Wednesday. These things upset my activity as a writer. What can I do, countess?

The COUNTESS sighs again.

COUNTESS: When my son comes back, he will take care of everything. (*She looks outside*) There's a crane on the roof of the woodshed.

INT. CASTLE AT DUX. DINGING ROOM. NIGHT.

The COUNT OF WALDSTEIN, young, lively, and witty, is finally back, with a party of FRIENDS. They all are young and full of life. Their dress is simple: the century is coming to an end; and with it has come the French Revolution. Neoclassicism is upon us. They are seated at a banquet, eating without too many niceties, speaking, and laughing.

COUNT: I'll introduce to you Giacomo Casanova, a celebrated adventurer. He's here these days, as my librarian.
GUESTS: Casanova? The one who fled the Piombi prison? He's said to be a great philanderer ... I thought he was dead ... He invented the lottery ... He must be a funny character ... Why, of course, let's see him ... I was told he's crazy.
COUNT (*shouts*): Come in, Giacomo! Come! We're waiting for you!

A silence full of curiosity grows. Slowly, CASANOVA enters. He's dressed in all his finery, with a powdered wig he wears an unbelievable old-fashioned getup. He looks like a peacock, a mask, a pathetic clown. The makeup can't cover the ruin of his seventy-year-old face.

He stops near the table and takes a bow worthy of a dancer. We hear some giggles.

CASANOVA moves forward taking small and graceful steps, in a triumph of velvet, feathers, rhinestones, and brocade. The contrast with the modern, simple style of the guests is striking. The guests keep quiet: they feel like laughing, but are frozen by a sense of pity.

CASANOVA, with the broad gestures of an old-fashioned mime, starts to declaim Ariosto's verses.

CASANOVA: His rage and fury mount to such a pitch
        They obfuscate and darken all his senses.
        Even his sword he leaves behind, from which
        It may be judged the mist of madness dense is.
        But neither sword nor scramasaxe so rich
        A crop could scythe; unarmed his strength immense is.
        Barehanded, he uproots at the first blow
        A tall and noble pine and lays it low.

CASANOVA mimes the madness of Orlando.

CASANOVA: And other pines, after the first, he pulls,
        As if so many fennel-stalks they were.
        Tall oak and seasoned elm likewise he culls,
        And beech and mountain ash and larch and fir . . .

The laughs, until now repressed, burst out among the GUESTS at his extremely ridiculous gestures. CASANOVA all of a sudden stops, glares all around with disappointment, reproach, scorn. He says nothing. He gives a bow and shaking, turns toward the door.

INT. CASTLE AT DUX. CASANOVA'S ROOM. NIGHT.

CASANOVA retires to his room, cluttered with papers, rolled up drawings, small statues, and rusty weapons. All his past has been accumulating, no longer with an order; it's a chaos of dusty memories, gnawed by mice. On the walls images of women, smiling ambiguously, stare at him as if to say goodbye. CASANOVA sits at his desk, and gazes into the space in front of him.

CASANOVA (*mutters*): I am proud because I am nothing.

He sniggers, as if he'd made a witty remark. He is absorbed in his thoughts and perhaps, drowsy. Then he rouses himself, assailed by a sudden thought.

CASANOVA: And Venice? Will I never go back to Venice?

CASANOVA gets up and walks to the window. And he sees . . .

EXT. VIEW FROM THE WINDOW. CASANOVA'S VISION. NIGHT.

. . . snow and a magnificent starry sky. Gradually the snow is transforming into the sea—the stormy sea of the Venetian lagoon. CASANOVA sees himself young, dressed as PIERROT. He's in a gondola rowing anxiously. Some other gondolas draw level with his. In each one is a woman of his past: HENRIETTE, MADDALENA, ANNAMARIA, the LITTLE GIRL from Vienna, LUCREZIA, LEONILDA, MADAM D'URFÉ, the GIANT WOMAN. Every gondola passes him. Every woman looks back and smiles to him for a last goodbye. Casanova's gondola remains behind. Lonely. And all around it's getting dark.

THE END.

About the Script

The most intriguing aspect of *Fellini's Casanova* is the metamorphosis from Giacomo Casanova's memoirs to Federico Fellini's screenplay, and from Fellini's screenplay to Fellini's film. In his memoirs, Casanova presents the story of his life in an exalted tone. "I have no pleasanter pastime than to converse with myself about my own affairs," he writes. He reveals that he was delighted with himself, sometimes even astonished looking at himself in the mirror. He describes proudly his "long career as a lover": "I was born for the sex opposite to mine . . . [and] did everything to make myself loved by it," he says. Recollections of his love affairs intertwine with descriptions of his financial manipulations, his gambling, his diplomatic missions, his occult interests, his meetings with famous contemporaries, and monarchs. He was recommended to the Prussian King, Frederick the Great, as a "singularly intelligent man, very capable in solving the most complicated problems and full of all manner of schemes." Casanova himself is convinced that he has a great mind, and that he, after all, is a creature of intelligence and talents, not just of the flesh.

Fellini disagrees. With very rare exceptions, in his screenplay and later in the film he presents Casanova only in romantic and sexual encounters, not even playing cards, although Casanova was an incurable gambler. This is no longer Casanova's self-indulgent and loving look at himself but Fellini's look at him—at times disrespectful, even sarcastic. At times Fellini makes fun of Casanova. In his interviews, Fellini called him "a completely external man without secrets and without shame, a presumptuous man . . . cumbersome as a horse in a house," but at times he feels sorry for him.

The screenplay predetermined an openly stylized presentation for the film—not a reenactment of the character's life, not an illusion of reality, so tempting in cinema, but rather something reminiscent of the circus or a variety show. Accordingly, the composition of *Fellini's Casanova* both in the screenplay and in the film is deliberately fragmented, a chain of independent "numbers"—groups of scenes united in sequences: Casanova's affair with the mysterious French woman, Henriette; Casanova in a Turkish nobleman's garden having a romantic encounter with the man; Casanova "taking care" of a little Viennese girl; Casanova's mysterious séances with Madam d'Urfé.

At the *exposition* of the screenplay, Casanova's voice introduces him over an empty, dark screen; in the *finale*, the old Casanova, visualizing himself as young again, sees the women of his life passing by him in gondolas and is ". . . lonely. And all around is getting dark." The beginning and the ending enfold the screenplay's sequences, the order of which is almost irrelevant because there is no unifying plot there. Only Casanova's occasional voice-over forms bridges between them. But *within* the sequences, we detect the traditional dramatic structure, with the beginning, middle, and end—and with the culmination of action and its resolution.

In the screenplay Fellini throws young Casanova into the chaos of the Venetian Carnival, with its noise, music, shouts from the crowd, and beating drums. Casanova, dressed in a white Pierrot costume, appears among puppets and maskers, Harlequins and Harlequinesses, Punches, Horses' Heads, Devils, and Dragons. A large white hat covers half of his heavily powdered white face:

> He is skipping and staggering, with a foolish gait. . . .
> A Harlequin, laughing, hits Casanova's head with his
> stick. Casanova-Pierrot turns, grabs him by his waist,
> lifts him up and hurls him to the ground. . . . The

maskers stop dancing . . . laughing, they throw themselves into the fray.

This is really a circus skit, and Casanova, dancing, tumbling, and fighting, acts like a *circus clown*. A little later, in his lovemaking scene with the nun, Maddalena, he is a *circus acrobat*; in the screenplay, Fellini remarks that the scene is "almost acrobatic, as in a circus." Still later, during Casanova's séances in Madame d'Urfé's laboratory, with its "mysterious pots and metal jars boiling on a stove and a black cat . . . coiled near the fire," he turns into a *circus magician*.

In numerous writings and interviews, Fellini repeatedly asserted that the circus was for him, from the first time he saw it as a child, a "prophesy," a prediction of his calling, "the annunciation made" to him. "The circus isn't just a show . . . it is a way of traveling through one's own life," Fellini emphasized.

He was especially fascinated with mystery of the clown, this

> . . . incarnation of a fantastic creature who expresses
> the irrational aspect of man; he stands for the
> instinct, for whatever is rebellious in each one of us
> and whatever stands up to the established order of
> things . . . The clown is a mirror in which man sees
> himself in a grotesque, deformed, ridiculous image. . . .

The circus atmosphere permeates the screenplay. Either *real* clowns are thrown into a scene (such as the Württemberg court sequence), or other characters, including Casanova, act *like* clowns, as in the skit with the huge "round as a ball" Barberina; she makes funny faces and sticks her tongue out at Casanova; she, with an "inspired air, releases a long, harmonious fart." Or the skit with Madame d'Urfé's undressing, "her endless garments falling, one after another, every time it seems to be finished, there is always another petticoat, vest, and panties." Such a familiar circus gag of exaggeration, the clown's *more, more,* still *more*! Or the number with Marcolina, the lover of Casanova's pitiful brother, the abbot. She slaps him. He cries, "she gives him another box on the ear." Casanova also slaps the abbot, who "disappears with a scream." Marcolina and Casanova close the door and make love, while the brother, in a lamentable voice, asks to be let in. These are traditional circus bits of mocker(s) and mocked, the clown's typical ruses: to rob, to bamboozle, to outwit.

The circus absurdity reaches its culmination in the sequence at Württemberg Castle, where the court clowns, the courtiers, and even the Duke himself behave as if they all were in a circus ring.

In his memoirs Casanova writes that the court of Württemberg was "the most brilliant . . . in all Europe," and that the Duke wanted no living ruler to be "more intelligent or more talented than he himself, or more accomplished in the art of inventing pleasures." The Duke didn't like to waste time. His courtiers were even instructed to wake him up after just three or four hours of night sleep.

All the documented facts are exaggerated and ridiculed in Fellini's screenplay: the stupid, purple-faced doctor; the courtiers who drag the Duke from his bed and throw him in a tub of ice-cold water; the awakening Duke who wants to hang everybody; the court singers and dancers who are transformed by Fellini into clowns and generously thrown into the scene.

When Casanova appears at the court, the Duke, taking him for one of his subjects, wants to hang him; meanwhile, one of the clowns strikes Casanova with the fake genitals. "Casanova . . . draws his sword, and strikes him with the flat of the blade. The clown falls backwards. Everyone laughs. Casanova smiles, satisfied." And even in describing the mechanical doll, the film beauty Rosalba, Fellini makes her face "painted broadly with red and black, *like a clown*." She is one of the Duke's treasures; another, the Duke brags, is a white monkey from the West Indies. "A horrible monkey," writes Fellini, "[it] fiercely bares its teeth, and is masturbating."

In the screenplay's Württemberg sequence, Fellini's grotesque attains its summit. Here the circus loses its playfulness and becomes frightening. In the film, the sequence is largely altered. The director deletes the horrible monkey, the clowns, the vulgar skits with the Duke, but carries over the prolific energy of the grotesque, with its piled-up absurdities: the Duke, now infantile, absent, immobile, listens to a seashell and is mesmerized by an enormous turtle; court musicians, dressed in military uniforms, frenziedly play huge organs as if attacking them (a mechanical act similar to Casanova's lovemaking); two officers are trying to lift up Rosalba's skirt; Casanova is talking about science; the court chorus is rhythmically booming. But above all this bizarre world soars the angelic voice of the chorus's soloist, and the sublime redeems the grotesque—Fellini's typical counterpoint of "textures" and emotions.

In the few scenes that are left in the screenplay after the Württemberg sequence, Fellini abruptly changes his attitude toward Casanova, and along with this the tone of the screenplay is changed too. Casanova, now Count Waldstein's librarian at the castle of Dux, is described as "lonely, old and shaky", a foreigner in shabby clothes, a Venetian in a Germanic country. He is distressed when he doesn't get his macaroni. The servants of the count, with whom he shares the table, despise and mock him: " . . . a sheet of paper with Casanova's portrait, stuck up on the lavatory's door and stained with excrement." The Count is absent, so Casanova seeks protection from his mother, the old Countess. Humbly, with tears in his eyes, he enters her room. In this scene Fellini's compassion overtakes his previous sarcasm. He feels sorry for Casanova. "It is not to indulge any whim that I come to you, but to beseech justice; justice for a *poor, old man* . . . " says Casanova. Departing from the dry conciseness of the screenplay genre, Fellini describes the scene in a free, poetic style:

> The Countess . . . is seated in an armchair near a window. Beyond the pane, divided in small rectangles, we catch sight of a stretch of snow, from which a few black, bare trees pop out. Even the old Countess is in some way skeleton-like and mournful; very pale, gaunt, she wears black and stares at the window wrapped in a sad meditation. She is a mournful image of the nearness of death (her death or Casanova's?)

She sighs; she cannot help him—she doesn't have the strength, doesn't know how, doesn't understand—and gazing outside, she tells him: "There is a crane on the roof of the woodshed."

What a subtext! What a sad indifference! Poor Casanova . . .

Compared to the screenplay, the number of scenes in the film was substantially reduced. It seems that when writing the script, Fellini didn't want to (or couldn't?) restrict himself. He once noted that the screenplay is like a suitcase you carry with you; you buy a lot of things on the way, and only sometime later, when the journey is over, do you realize which ones are really needed. Among the scenes edited out of the screenplay (some for financial considerations) were Casanova's meeting with Voltaire; the scenes with the Austrian Empress Maria Theresa; the episode in Turkey; the scene of Casanova spending a passionate night with his own daughter, Leonilda; and numerous others.

The structure in the film is much tighter than it is in the screenplay. Although the sequences are still somewhat disjointed in terms of plot, nevertheless, the unity of the film is achieved, first of all, through the dynamic of the visual composition. The film starts with a dazzling carnival at the Grand Canal in Venice; it ends at the same place, only now the canal is frozen and Casanova glides across its surface in a slow waltz with the mechanical doll, Rosalba. Through the film there occurs a gradual dimming of color—from intense, brazen colors at the beginning to transparent, dissolving, and disappearing "watercolors" at the end—such an unintrusive metaphor for the extinguishing of life, for coming to the end.

The unity of *Fellini's Casanova* is also strengthened by recurring themes that run through and hold together the film's "vignettes": *performers and performances*; *successes and failures*; *dolls, puppets, and puppeteers*. These themes, like the musical themes of Nino Rota's score for the film, continually transpose and vary. Most of them originated in the screenplay but were further developed, shaped, enriched, and fully realized in the film., For example, in the script, the theme of *performers and performances* was played out mainly in the circus mode. In the film it was replaced by and expanded into other types of performances with a much richer variety of moods and meanings: puppets on stilts in the opening carnival scene; a duet of castrati at the hunch-back Du Bois's party in Parma; a fragment of *Orpheus and Eurydice* presented at the theater in Dresden; the giantess's show in London. For us, the film audience, the *performers* and *their audience* are equally interesting. So, when Du Bois, sparkling and iridescent in his dragon-fly costume, sings and dances with his male partner and they mime lovemaking, the reactions of his guests—the prim Spaniards ("It's scandaloso!") and the light-minded, cheerful, giggling French—are no less entertaining.

Casanova is also a *performer*. When he makes love to the nun, Mad-dalena, to entertain a voyeur, the French ambassador, the latter exclaims: "Excellent performance. . . . Brava! Well done!" But Casanova's main number, although masterful, is repetitious and devoid of emotions, like the mechanical rhythmic stirring and flutter-ing of his clockwork bird he always carries with him. Casanova-per-former has his successes, such as his competition in lovemaking with a coachman at Lord Tallow's palace in Rome, where Casanova is the tri-umphant winner. But he has humiliating failures also. When two women push him out of their carriage, spitting in his face and calling him "impotent old man," he is ready to commit suicide. Or his other, final failure: now an old man—or rather an old dressed-up doll in laces and silk, mechanically pounding his staff and bowing theatri-cally—he recites Ariosto for his patron, Count Waldstein, and the Count's young guests, who cannot help laughing at Casanova. This is any performer's nightmare, and probably the film director's too: to be out of date, out of place, to hear your audience making fun of you, and to realize that your time has passed.

"What sort of a crazy inventor was your father," Casanova asks the doll, Rosalba, as he undresses her and examines her mechanism. "He must have been a poet as well, because he made you so beautiful . . . ." In a way, this inventor was Fellini himself. He created this character—there was no Rosalba in Casanova's memoirs. From the screenplay to the film, Rosalba undergoes a remarkable transformation. In the film there is no trace of her "blank gaze" or of her face "painted red and black like a clown." Now she is a beauty, the only one who remains in Casanova's dreams until the very end. They dance on the ice of a frozen Venetian lagoon, and even the pope, riding past in a gilded carriage along with Casanova's mother, points approvingly at Rosalba. Casanova and the doll, close together and remarkably alike, turn again and again in their slow waltz.

Fellini, the puppet master, as he often called himself, gently hints that in this film dolls and people have an innate closeness: dummies in the dressmaker's shop "here and there lift their heads, which are bald or adorned with wigs," and the pale girl Annamaria, "white as wax, . . . [is] standing still, . . . keeping her eyes closed . . . beautiful statue." Even Casanova's mother (he meets her accidentally in the Dresden theater), looks like an old doll whose mechanism is broken; she cannot walk.

From the screenplay to the film, Fellini developed the images of dolls, statues, and puppets. In a way, they are related not only to the clockwork doll Rosalba but also to the puppetlike Casanova.

And then there is Henriette, whom Fellini in the screenplay calls "an 18th century statuette." In the film, even the director succumbs to her charms: Fellini adorns her with a porcelain-pink dress and white wig; he makes her smile bewitching and her cello playing sweetly sad. And while Casanova weeps with joy over having met this "divine woman," Fellini, the puppeteer, knows that in a moment she will disappear, and it seems he *himself* is missing her already.

One of the most telling changes from the screenplay to the film is in the image of the giantess. In the screenplay she is described as

> almost an *elephant.* She holds the hand of a small man, who is leading her like a *beast* . . . [she] stops at the water's edge, spreads her huge legs and pees with the strength of a *horse* . . . [she] opens her mouth in a sinister smile: she is missing two front teeth.

In the film she has a gentle smile, a big, kind face, and an angelic name—Angelina.

In the screenplay Casanova is "enchanted, curious, and attracted" to this "extraordinary" woman, a circus wrestler, who defeats all men who dare to challenge her, including Casanova. But he, following his defeat, seduces her. "I am in love with you . . . I adore you," he says. They "hug, kiss, and make love . . . ."

In the film he is also enchanted by her, but she is unattainable. She is not only stronger than he, she is also taller, *larger*. She is unspoiled. Casanova is no match for her. He spends the night *outside* her tent, able only to peek timidly through a hole in the canvas at her childlike happiness as Angelina, humming a lullaby ("Pnin-Pinin-Valen-tin, Valen-tin . . ."), carefully handles her dolls, one at a time, and plays with her living dolls—the two dwarves. It seems that here, Fellini, the puppeteer, who admitted that he always "falls in love with [his] puppets—[his] actors and characters, and takes care of them," identifies with Angelina. We can go even further and say that she, to an extent, is Fellini's self-portrait. He, if only for a moment, disguises himself as the giantess; the way Rembrandt disguised himself as a guard in his *The Night Watch*, or Picasso, as a Harlequin in his *The Acrobat's Family*.

Inga Karetnikova